Fishing *with* Hope

CHRIS OWEN

Ark House Press
arkhousepress.com

Some names and identifying details have been changed to protect the privacy of individuals.

Cataloguing in Publication Data:
Title: Fishing With Hope
ISBN: 978-1-7646163-6-2 (pbk)
Subjects: REL012170 RELIGION / Christian Living / Personal Memoirs; REL012040 RELIGION / Christian Living / Inspirational.

Design by initiateagency.com

TABLE OF CONTENTS

INTRODUCTION

This book is based on true stories that still echo through the ages. As I look back and share these revelations that have changed the course of my life and led me on a journey that shaped who I have become, I open the pages of both the past and present, still deeply forged in my memory.

These memories, as I wind back the clock, reveal the true nature of the serious events that played a significant role in causing deep damage within me. These experiences are drawn from my own life, as I share moments that capture the true meaning of a misfortunate series of events. From early childhood, these times did not portray a picture-perfect world, but rather a dark and confronting reality. As I pull back the curtain, I revisit those life-changing experiences that produced heartache and pain, revealing a deeper darkness that influenced my entire life.

As I share this testimony with you, my hope is that you may find truth and answers to life's deeper questions. Perhaps the right key will unlock understanding—helping you make sense of a damaged heart that moulds one's character, where reality and justice seem to cry out for relief on this journey of hope.

In this world, where the intelligent, the educated and the rulers of this age stand, all their wisdom can never truly challenge lived experience. When something is tried and proven, experience will always triumph over philosophy. A personal testimony stands as evidence of something real—a true miracle. Otherwise, I would struggle to believe that I am here by chance, with no purpose or design. If time passes and nothing meaningful materialises in my life, where do I stand? Do I simply follow the forces of nature and do what seems natural in the order of things? Surely life must be more than a series of events, waiting for a miracle to happen in the search for meaning, where one longs to discover their purpose for living. This raises the question: who will I serve, and who will be my beacon of light as I carry this flaw that can never measure up to a moral standard in this arena of life and death? If I do not regard my life as important or as having a reason for living, it creates a moral dilemma. And when all fails, it becomes easy to give up on life. But perhaps I am valued far more than I realise, and by entrusting my life to a greater power, it can be turned into something beautiful.

When you uncover one's cruelty in the passing age and begin to discover hidden lies, it reveals that many things are not what they seem. You come to realise that the heavy burden you carry was not an accident, and you begin to question life itself. What did I see, steal, kill or lie about? Who sowed and programmed this perverted ideology within me, shaping it into a common trait and feeding me a false perception of life? This inner battle only adds to the confusion, as evil operates behind the scenes to manipulate and distort a person's natural life into something unnatural. It draws in easy targets, inviting them into its schemes and programming them into submission, ultimately driving them towards destructive behaviour. When one becomes entangled in traditions and the ways of man, it brings doubt and uncertainty, especially for a wounded person trying to find their way forward.

There are no guarantees in life, but one thing is certain—failure and discouragement often loom large, with the promise of bad news at every turn. Whether we like it or not, no one leaves this world alive. Everything has an expiry date, no matter one's position. We live in a world marked by chaos and disorder, offering no true solution or substitute for a better life. As long as power and greed sit behind false promises, this remains the reality. This world, under the sway of evil, promises pleasure and comfort, yet seeks to capture the soul—drawing people into illusion and replacing truth with make-believe. What appears harmless is often misleading, designed to entice the vulnerable into a false sense of security and lead them into immorality. These influences shape perception, behaviour and ultimately character.

The world's view rarely reveals the hidden cost of hardship and failure. Instead, it presents a façade, offering opportunity and promise. Naturally, not knowing any different, people are drawn into this system, believing there is hope to be found within it.

Yet, like most things, truth eventually reveals itself. What once seemed good can quickly unravel, leaving a person awakened and disoriented, as all their effort, time and plans come to a halt. Beliefs begin to crumble. You call out for help, yet the world, despite its wisdom and knowledge, offers little in return. It cannot provide the answers you seek or offer lasting relief. However you look at it, you are left alone, trying to piece your life back together and find closure for the wounds you carry. Trust in those in authority fades, leaving confusion and a deep longing for something that can truly satisfy the soul.

At its core, human nature is fragile—searching, curious and often driven to fill the void within. People take ideas or obsessions and turn them into a means of gain, pursuing happiness in whatever form they can. Yet no matter the outcome, the principle of life remains unchanged: what you sow, you will reap. Nothing is hidden from God, and in time, all things are brought into account.

Every form of corruption leaves its mark, staining the soul and leaving deep wounds that can linger for a lifetime. These wounds are often accompanied by painful memories, making it difficult to function fully within society.

As a result, many seek professional help, searching for comfort and support in the hope of finding freedom. Yet often, they are labelled by the experts of this world as dysfunctional or abnormal, diagnosed and treated with man-made solutions that offer only temporary relief. Beneath the surface, however, lies a deeper root—a wound that has shaped identity and produced ongoing suffering. True healing requires more than temporary solutions; it calls for a deeper restoration of the heart.

CHAPTER 1
Let The Show Begin

This story had started long ago, from the time of childhood, where history played a major part throughout time in bringing these misfortunate incidents for one to inherit through a series of events, giving you a bad start in life and creating a sad story about a simple boy born into a large family, who one day fell to a horrific tragedy that struck us down with the sting of war. This sudden disaster had dramatically changed our way of living and forced us to quickly switch from normal to survival mode, causing us to rearrange our lifestyle and shift to take what was at hand. It left us helpless, in a desperate state of shock, having to look for a way out. With no regard for civil rights, we became victims of the acts of war.

This kind of tragedy can instantly snatch your hopes and dreams right before your eyes. It can leave you feeling stranded and abandoned, losing out to the evil schemes of man and leaving you contemplating what will happen in the silent years that hold your future.

This experience does so many things to a person on so many levels. It can transform and affect every area of your soul, leaving nothing pleasant to consider, where it concerns the natural and spiritual combined, creating a solitary condition and a bruised heart with one devastating blow. This disorder will eventually produce bad symptoms over time during your life and will begin to show in the outworking of your body, health and mental state, being embedded in you. Evil does not take a holiday; it roams around looking for a target to hold captive and imprison.

Where can one turn from this mind-boggling experience that was hard to comprehend by its logic? It left me with a sick feeling of uncertainty for the future. This, happening at an early age, left nothing to be desired. When you're caught up in the middle of war and trying to cope with the sound and graphics of war on display, having no assurance for tomorrow.

As the war intensified and danger was closing in, we could no longer reside in our current place; we had to find a safe place. Escaping, we drove around looking to take cover, to avoid the danger of being killed.

It was hard for a little boy to understand what was happening around him, watching the graphic scenes of turmoil and collapsing ruins and wreckage that spoke of life and death. With every passing image, leaving you numb and empty inside, with so many questions running through your head. What will remain and what will become of us? As this reality leaves you to ponder your next moment, when you reluctantly gaze into this vast sky of homeland.

The danger was increasing all around us. We had no option but to escape from being caught in a crossfire and become a statistic. It was common sense; we needed to head to a place of refuge. We had to take risks, knowing this was no easy task, crossing the borderline. We watched intently, going through the military boundary checkpoint and drive-through. It was either take a chance or stay behind and risk it all. This left us no choice. Being one family cramped in a vehicle, we slowly approached the soldiers on duty. They asked us to provide documentation as proof of residence to pass through. The confrontation kept us still and quiet in the moment. The soldiers were satisfied with the papers being in order, so they waved us through.

With relief, we continued our travel, heading towards the village where our grandma and uncles lived in a safe zone. This was our only hope and way out for a better life, staying with our relatives.

The drive wasn't long. As we approached the village, my curiosity got the better of me. Looking intently at this strange and beautiful green land, surrounded by plenty of fruit trees. There were adventures laid to discover; a little boy to wander in this natural habitation and a place full of exciting things to explore.

There were no complaints from any of my siblings. We all loved this amazing place and began to enjoy our time there, without a care in the world, making friends and playing games, watching the seasons roll by. For such a time, we made it work, living together. Fifteen of us sleeping on the floor. The adults had a role to fulfil, like preparing the food from the inhabitants of the earth, with tasks like bathing us in a production line: strip, wash, dry, dress and move out.

When you're in a happy place, time is not a factor. We didn't even notice time passing away so quickly, as the years rolled by.

During our stay there, a strange behaviour was noticed by my uncles. They suspected a case of abuse had taken place. This serious matter had got them all stirred up. An explanation was necessary for this absurd behaviour that was improper and evil in their eyes. They observed that this situation was damaging, dangerous and disgusting.

This situation was life-threatening, where the victim did not deserve this kind of treatment in the age of innocence. So, by confronting the guilty party and bringing this pattern of secrecy to his attention, it needed to come out in the open. For it involved the disappearance of a child for a time and the child had returned confused.

This had caused an uproar and an altercation between Dad and his brothers over this criminal act and hidden scheme for profit. Dad had to be held accountable for his actions.

The arguments went back and forth with no explanation. As a result, Dad, in his stubbornness and extreme temper, would not acknowledge his wrongdoing. The uncles vigorously voiced their views that this behaviour was not to be tolerated or accepted among the community. The only thing he could do was to pack us all up in rage and drive us back to Beirut, forcing us to live with his sister (his accomplice), who was a widow and lived on the third floor of a building with her children. She accommodated us with her charm and deception and her role-play acting. There was nothing pretty about this place and its hollow surroundings that echoed with war.

This dumb idea was to simply throw us in the lion's den, like a sitting duck becoming a target for the enemy in a dangerous war zone area, with no means of communication or protection available in sight.

His behaviour and decision-making in such hostility, to relocate us in the worst position, showed no regard for his children and spoke volumes about his actions that only proved he had no remorse or care for our safety. He was an absent and heartless father, who was filled with pride and anger. This demonstrated his character, even toward his own children, playing the secret agent with a hidden agenda and parading around while leaving Mum to manage the children, and would beat her up if she dared ask.

The contrast in this place was the complete opposite compared to the sweet aroma of the village. Here the sound of bombing and firing echoed day and night, getting louder and stronger, with no way out. You could feel it getting closer, as it made us feel helpless and scared, knowing we were stuck in this building with no escape or help to defend us or our surrounding neighbours in this forsaken town. As the danger drew nearer, not knowing what would happen next, we were in a state of chaos that determined our future had relied on a miracle in wait, while listening to the sound of war approaching the town.

As it got louder, suddenly, in a quick flash, there was a loud explosion that erupted in the town and landed near our vicinity. This bomb sent shock waves through the neighbourhood.

Upon hearing this deafening noise (that was alarming and disturbing for all to hear in its form), in that instant, shouts of crying followed dramatically, where death had struck the people and silence hovered over the area.

On hearing this howling, Mum reacted quickly and went into protection mode and directed us to move over to the other side of the house and hide behind the wall from the danger. Not understanding what was going on or the severity of it all, we all sat there quietly, waiting and listening to the firing and explosions going off.

This bombardment all happened in one motion. Consequently, Dad and his sister were standing by the window, facing the bomb side of the building, looking out for signs of danger. Then, without warning, a loud thundering explosion shook the building. Before anyone could react, in a split second, a wave of shells had blown through the window of the room where Dad was standing. Upon hearing this frightening sound, the shattering explosion caused a sudden terror that consumed everyone with the fear of death. This terrifying blast had gripped us with uncertainty while sitting in silence and a state of shock.

In that very moment, a loud scream of hysteria came from Mum as she witnessed this devastating act of disbelief. She watched Dad walk towards us, holding his neck to stop the blood from gushing out. He took his last step and fell dead on the ground. Some pieces of the shells also claimed a second person, our aunty, who was found dead on the kitchen floor.

In watching this horrific death experience that had just overwhelmed everyone with fear, it was a misfortunate disaster that had occurred right in front of our eyes. A tragedy hard to swallow, where emotions had been stunned by this cruel blow. One couldn't imagine the effect it had on us, not being able to grasp what had just struck us, where everyone broke out in cries.

But for some reason regarding this event, mixed feelings arose within me, not utterly saddened by this death experience. Most likely it may have been a combination of both emotions — the shock and bad relationship with Dad didn't register at the time.

Meanwhile, this incident didn't go unnoticed. Nearby neighbours knew what happened and came to our rescue. They brought comfort and support during this painful time, gathering and helping to remove the dead bodies.

When I look back on this mysterious event that took place, I find it interesting how this had occurred, in raising the elementary question, what's it all mean? "What was the purpose of their death; a coincidence or a punishment for their deeds?"

Of course, this argument is open for interpretation. This doesn't change the fact that this family of loss had suffered a major blow where the chain of events lay in wait.

The reality now meant that the main provider had gone, leaving a family behind to manage financially and emotionally. To survive this new change in a world of struggle, we had to begin to search for other means to sustain us during this hectic time, where the supply of food became a desperate cry. Mum now had an even greater responsibility, to somehow provide and care for her nine children on her own.

When the going gets tough, the tough get going. Desperate times call for desperate measures. Our extraordinary Mum rose to the challenge and began to find ways through various means, by baking bread, sourcing whatever food was available to feed us during those hard times in a town occupied by the military force.

As the days of struggle rolled by, the war began to slightly ease off. This gave us a chance to find whatever was necessary to help keep us alive, to manage while waiting for help to arrive.

This tragic news had made its way through familiar connections and reached Dad's brothers in the village. As soon as they found out what happened, they quickly acted, without hesitation, and responded to the call. Realising the critical state of our position, being surrounded by danger on every side, they immediately came to our rescue. One of our nice uncles volunteered to take the risk and the sacrifice on our behalf, knowing what was involved. In a volatile country that's occupied by the enemy, he was determined to save us at any cost. Through careful routes of danger, he finally reached us. It was a welcoming sight, seeing his loving face of compassion that was willing to help and lead us to safety at an appropriate time.

This was not an easy situation to accomplish. The way out of this place required careful planning, without causing a scene which could end up badly. We were determined to leave this forsaken town that was left in ruins and heartache.

So, we waited patiently for our brave uncle to plan our escape, with his skill and understanding of the situation, to complete this mission.

Meanwhile, we would go about our business and continue to source out our daily bread.

I still remember when uncle and I walked the empty, quiet streets of ruin that were guarded by soldiers, needing to reach certain people to donate food. I, being so little, could only observe my uncle as we walked along the path. He took me along as a distraction to discourage any sudden danger when stopped by a soldier. As we confronted a postal guard, uncle would greet him by offering him a cigarette. This gesture of respect would eliminate any suspicion in their mind from creating an unfriendly scene.

As the days rolled by, the opportunity of leaving and returning to the village had become a reality, where once again we would feel safe and free in a place of happiness and away from this danger. We packed our essentials and headed for Grandma's, a place where we would be surrounded by good company and great caring people.

We arrived at Grandma's place with a heart of gratitude. Everyone greeted and welcomed us with open arms. They understood the gravity of the situation that had arisen and were very concerned about our safety. They were delighted to see us and ready to comfort our broken hearts.

This was not an easy time for all of us, to get together considering the circumstances, in dealing with the loss and the unfortunate hardship that came about. Mum, in her weakness and pain, was able to release and share her heartache with the family, explaining what took place as she witnessed the traumatic, painful and agonising death of her husband. As this took a toll on her, the family were in full support and admiration of her willingness to endure such a horrific event. They were able to bring comfort and relief at this devastating time.

For us kids, it was hard to understand everything that had just happened. Trying to grasp the meaning of this would be overwhelming, to see the overall picture of this loss. If any consolation, we were just glad to be back, roaming the village with freedom.

As the days turned into weeks and weeks into months, the year had passed by very quickly, especially whilst we were having fun. But being in this position, that didn't last forever. Something was brewing as some news had been brought to our attention. We discovered that we were going to move to a different country, making for a better life. For the war had made survival virtually impossible to raise a family in this country, particularly for a widow to raise nine children on her own. We took the news with mixed feelings. On hearing the idea, it was exciting to start over in another country that promised a better life, where Mum had her immediate family residing there. This was the best solution for our future.

So, the process had begun. Mum and uncles started making plans to prepare our migration settlement. Its official change was in the air and in motion. Everybody was working together to organise the necessary documentation, such as passports, and raise money by selling whatever goods and possessions we had to reach our goal.

This exhausting plan took about two years to come together. Everyone involved did their part and continually stayed in communication with our Australian relatives, who were organising the sponsorship for residency.

One would assume this would be no easy task, having to deport a family of ten across the ocean and into a foreign land, especially having no understanding or concept of its history and culture.

We had no idea what to expect, nor could we speak English. Mum was a fighter, a tower of strength. She was determined to do this at any cost, daring to carry her nine children across the ocean.

As time drew nearer, arrangements were made. A travel guide would assist us on this migrating journey. We called on a superhero to accompany us along the way, who had the understanding and skills to fly us out. This person of bravery was full of courage and took a risk to help others in need, by offering his service to protect and ensure a safe arrival at our destination.

This selfless, caring man, being our uncle on Mum's side, met us for the first time, a helpless broken family.

And so, the journey began. It was time to depart. As the trip became a reality, as the day approached, excitement and sadness arose. It stirred your emotions, where the tear of separation poured out in the dying fade of the last wave goodbye, leaving our kinfolk behind, who showed us love and support, to finally watch us disappear in the distant clouds.

There was so much to contemplate as we took this painful trip of escape to a different country, a foreign land of uncharted waters. This left you questioning your future, after all that happened and having to carry that empty feeling inside. When you were stripped down to nothing, it made you wonder about life, as you carried a suitcase full of broken dreams, not knowing what tomorrow brings.

This was the ultimate challenge for us. But if there was any virtue of excellence, I've learnt over the years from watching my mother resist defeat, she showed us that humans can become fearless and resilient when it comes to survival. They seem to find strength and courage in times of trouble and rise to the challenge to overcome the impossible.

One can understand that a reluctant move is a very difficult and painful task for a fatherless family, to somehow pick up the remaining pieces and start over again in times of brokenness, especially when you lose a father in a meaningless war and leave behind nine children with a hole to fill for a widowed mother.

This kind of burden can overwhelm anyone. This picture I'm drawing here is not a famous work of art; it portrays sadness and sorrow worn by a mother. She is the feature of the story here, how she was left to carry a heavy load of misfortune by herself. If you looked closely at her face, you would have seen the swelling in her eyes, which displayed the ache in her heart through those desperate times.

Mum had determined in her heart that there was no going back. She sadly accepted the fact, taking on a new role and responsibility to solely raise her children, to push through the pain, wanting to give them a better life.

My amazing mum single-handedly defied the odds that weighed up against the measuring scale of motherhood. She super-exceeded any expectation of any parent guidebook. Her love and sacrifice were worth their weight in gold, as she faced the limitations and hardships of life.

My mum deserved more than a medal of honour or an achievement award for her accomplishments, but the greater superseded the latter. All she asked in return for her reward was to see her children achieve greatness in the land of the living.

CHAPTER 2

Final Destination - New Beginnings

Trying to grasp this new beginning was mind-boggling for me, as thoughts ran around in my head about leaving the past behind. What does it all mean and what will become of us now? We finally left the place that presented us with an ugly outcome that brought havoc and chaos.

This flight was about to mark a new beginning for us, a whole new era to rewrite. Coming out of the old and stepping into the new. To embark on a new territory and come into our destination. Life was about to take on a whole new meaning, a new chapter. To finally reach our last stop and land our feet on this ground, where we can create a new history for ourselves, when we touch the soil of this great nation of opportunity.

As the plane landed, mixed feelings began to stir in my heart, rejoicing and celebrating the final stop, leaving our troubles behind.

We got picked up from the airport and headed towards our new rental property that had been provided for us. As we drove into the land, my curiosity began to arouse. As I watched and observed the scenery that caught my eye, I began to think about my future in this strange new world I would call home. It was hard to digest this new change and come to terms with it, to accept a better world that was open for greater things.

This new country, Australia, would bring many challenges and tests. I would have to make new adjustments to understand this cultural place and its ways. The equation was simply, I had to accept this change to learn and grow, by taking the good with the bad. What followed from here would determine my future, where certain challenges would confront and test me on this path of life. Many life experiences would bring understanding and knowledge to help develop my maturity.

To start the learning system, enrolment in school was essential for an eight-year-old boy. I was placed in primary school. Being out of school for so long, I fell behind. Now, a foreigner who spoke no English, I had to fight for social acceptance. The language barrier played a whole new song of cruelty in a strange country that left little room for comfort as an outsider.

This form of lifestyle in a different culture was unfamiliar to me. I struggled to adjust and adapt to its customs and traditions. It was a frustrating uphill battle that clashed with my upbringing. Having nothing to prove, I just wanted to be accepted without the heroic reputation syndrome.

This new life needed to suit my personality. I was someone who would avoid conflict and not entangle with the affairs of this world for what it represented. I preferred to let life gradually evolve around my own environment of familiarity, at a pace of a slow and steady process, where education and common ground would meet in a socially safe environment.

Naturally, you could never predict the outcome of any situation. It is not possible to have a fireproof plan. There's no such thing as a perfect world. You quickly learn that things don't go according to plan. Life is not perfect, as you learn the hard way by your current situation. Living in a rough town is not the ideal place for raising a family. It was like being thrown in a battlefield, having to fight your way out. These ongoing episodes brought us so many painful memories of trouble and hardship, where the heart grew faint and was made to bear a multitude of scars. If there was one thing I'm sure of, it is that hurt and pain don't take a holiday.

From what I observed, people here have a lot of freedom and comforts compared to third-world countries, that's open for disaster. This can build this kind of human behaviour, where one can easily get entangled in it. As a family, we put up with it for a season, where the signs of relocating towns were in motion. It was common knowledge to us and time was drawing near to farewell this place of cultural war.

When the day had finally come to relocate towns, these were happy days for us, where celebration was in order, gladly desiring to leave this awful place that offered nothing but emotional damage to the family.

It was a case of a misfortune of events that affected our sanity in the long term and changed our perception on life. When the family were exposed to such a hostile environment, we wished we had never encountered these kinds of people, but I quickly learned that life doesn't promise you a bed of roses. Life can certainly throw at you these unforeseen adversities. It makes you wonder why human nature is so corrupt. Consequently, because of these people's behaviour and actions, I was tossed back and forth like a wave that carried these scars with its deep roots that lay unsettled inside. Of course, I could conclude that problems, depending on your situation, can produce heartache that tends to grip you emotionally and spiritually. One horrific event can set you up for a downfall and take you for a ride on a course with the flow-on effect of a hopeless life.

One can easily inherit these deficiencies into adulthood and the venom that evil produces can shape and mould your identity to transform you into an ugly duckling, slowly aiming to consume and sear your conscience to dead works by convincing you to believe the lie. This false persuasion tends to convert you into becoming a lost soul, with its harmful characteristics that keep you bound up and avoid any personal confrontation that could expose the truth. In any circumstance, you are driven by this confusion and rather tend to choose the easy way out when it comes to talking about your inner deep hurts. It is always easier to escape to a comforting place with a familiar setting, which calms your pain, where no one can stir the pot and you have to face it.

Human nature would rather ignore and avoid the past and look for temporary relief to forget the ugly experience, living on the edge and relying on time to heal all wounds. Hoping that a new method would find a solution somehow and make it mind over matter, but after many trials you discover things don't just disappear by themselves.

When you take a good look at yourself, you discover there are more deep things hidden and covered internally in the passing years, which have produced this nature you possess in the outworkings of your personhood. The signs you develop prove you lack confidence and maturity when desiring to fit into society and an unfamiliar environment. It took a lot of internal searching and self-convincing for me to decide to take a stand with courage on the inner battles of struggle and use whatever tool or knowledge I've gained over time to be able to fit into this jungle of survival.

CHAPTER 3
Share And Dare

Sometimes you need to do something about it or take action to achieve your goals. Having this knowledge, you will find out more about yourself. This way of living has opened my eyes to the unforeseen world of lies, as I share my heart to explain the things which I inherited and changed my life. I'm sure many people can relate to a painful and suffering experience, especially when you become a victim of circumstances you didn't sign up for. Life sure has a way of taking a turn for the worse. It wasn't by choice or self-inflicted; rather, I was forced to adopt the painful scars of abuse at a young age. This undeserved treatment would alter my destiny and ultimately prepare me for the long, widening road of hardship.

To carry a heavy load, wicked intent had sucked the life out of my innocent heart, leaving me with no reassurance, only to be accompanied by battle scars that weighed me down to fall on the wrong end of the scale. In the scheme of things, where the actual perpetrator, having no regard for my innocence or sanity, deliberately and purposely used me for his own self-gain. This experience left me paralysed, where justice meant nothing in the eyes of the deceiver.

Where did I stand when life became unfair? The burdens of distasteful memories took their toll on my quality of life, where darkness accompanied me, clouded my journey and displayed signs that robbed my freedom on the trail of no hope. This dark world left me wearing scars that damaged my heart in this evil situation that was forcefully handed to me.

The irony of it all was, no matter how you look at it, the act of evil stands, however you try to comprehend this defining moment that changed the course of life. It left an innocent person scrambling for survival in a state of shock, or searching for answers, to understand the meaning of this devious act that took place. It was so hard to make sense of it all. You come to wonder if this thing was by design or part of a scheme of darkness at work to cause destruction in your life. You can't make this stuff up. It's so real that it makes you quiver, knowing this act of cruelty was committed by nature, when having to revisit it in the awakening of a new dawn.

Being through it all and being alive today is surely an act of a divine miracle from my point of view. As I look back now, I can see God was with me, helping me get through the ordeal. I can't blame Him for my misfortunes or crises. This knowledge comes when you open the eyes of your understanding to see the big picture and not what you consume or believe to be true. With age, you learn not everything is what it seems when you search deeper.

This principle can work for someone in their time of struggle. To take a deep look at your case and consider the possibilities of its nature and root cause, where the environment that was created for you has a significant reason for this condition that makes you aware. This will determine the source where the problem lies and, by linking it back to where it originated from, can bring freedom.

Wrong actions and bad decisions can have serious consequences, depending on the violation committed. They can become a stumbling block that trips you up through the ages and steers you in the wrong direction. They leave you with those inner hurts to bear, all the while because of the damage done, they can act as a coping mechanism when dealing with similar issues, and act as a shield to avoid confrontation. These things play a big part in our lives, for whatever reason they were inherited during life. They can go right back to an environment or influential upbringing and can leave a mark or stain on our soul.

Every setback and wrongdoing can sometimes be traced back to our childhood, where misconduct and misfortune can play a big part in the lessons of life, in the way we perceive things in our generation, that can mould and shape humans to adopt certain ideas, habits and values that shape one's character. They tend to follow their cultural and traditional ideology that binds them together, but what it may cause externally through the spiritual and outworking in the natural remains to be seen.

Many false common denominators can be justifiable and reasonable, based on a person's beliefs, regardless of their background. They will swear by it and testify to it, that what they are doing is right and it works for them. They will use the evil side in ignorance to satisfy their own cravings and selfish desires and are convinced that the greater pleasure is worth it.

I was once snared by this false perception in not knowing the capabilities of human nature, as an innocent child that had no concept or idea that such evil existed on a large scale, where one would practise such filth and behaviour and offer financial incentives to the supplier. During this extraordinary encounter, I happened to become a prisoner of sabotage. As a vulnerable little boy, I was left to defend for myself with little resistance or escape, where the ritual acts of deception and scare tactics convinced me to believe through fear that evil was my friend. I was thrown to the vultures into a dungeon of unbearable torment that continued to operate in the scheme of destruction. In the interim, these scavengers would convert and initiate recruits by disregarding the greater importance which took precedence over my life.

It was hard enough to endure hardship in a country where you fell victim to a crippling war of devastation on so many agonising levels. As you can imagine, this kind of impact had a rippling effect on my life. How can you compare this kind of suffering, when survival was the main priority? Everything else seemed dim in the scheme of things and all the signs pointed to defeat. Everything else around you was constantly changing in a twinkle of an eye. You suddenly watch your world turn upside down as the sirens of war shape your destiny. This is not a memory you want to capture as a child through this disaster, where everything came to a halt and caused an entire community to stop and take shelter. This included the closure of businesses and schools, where learning had stopped at a young age, putting education on hold. You could say I took a very long recess.

In these heartbreaking crises, there were so many decisions and survival techniques to consider by families that required serious attention for safety first. Being caught up in the crossfire of ruins, this life-changing moment had a dramatic effect on your survival mode, to staying alive and watching and listening to the sounds of hopelessness that surround you. The war would only intensify, leaving no room for other possibilities.

CHAPTER 4
First Real Job

To share these views of my traumatic events that revert to childhood and flow on to adulthood, they have consequently reshaped my life and the current state of my condition, to somehow function in a world that offers no handouts or apology for mishaps or misfortunate incidents. This you need to figure out and come to terms with the idea that it is necessary to make some adjustments that enable you to partake in social life and the workforce in order to survive.

So, the challenge began. It was time to take responsibility and make something of myself. This course required waiting and anticipating what life handed me and unfolded in due time.

Timing is an amazing thing; when something is meant to be, it just falls into place, which is part of the greater plan for your life.

This occurrence just happened as it aligned itself on one perfect day, when I joined up with friends in the city for fun. This was no ordinary day. It was orchestrated that I would connect with a specific person, who apparently was set on applying for an office job. This opportunity happened to catch my attention and I felt inspired to do the same. So, I nervously submitted my application and left it in the hands of opportunity.

This day was enthralling and, as a result, birthed a new feeling in me, leaving me to ponder that night as I contemplated on my bed the possibility of entering the workplace that consisted of an office environment. Would it be more satisfying than a factory job? So many thoughts ran through my head that night, lying there and thinking about life and the setback of lacking the skill, education and knowledge I possessed. This scary giant step was beyond my capability and I didn't qualify for it, but I was willing and determined to take a chance. I did the next best thing that night. I decided to call out to a greater power and ask God for help in this time of desperation and left it at that.

A week later, I received a phone call from the company involved, inviting me for an interview regarding a vacancy available for the temporary position. This exciting news was the first step in going forward towards a real job, and after that, the nervous phone call. I let this opportunity sink in, which was incredible to believe that this good fortune had come my way.

The date was set in motion and, having time to reflect on the nature of the role, it was a whole new dimension to my understanding. I was willing to attend the interview regardless of the outcome.

So, the day had arrived for my greatest test, to see where I stood and how this meeting would turn out. I entered the building and presented myself to the receptionist and sat down to be called in. Shortly after that, I was next on the list and was motioned to go in. Introductions were made with polite gestures before the interview began. Then the person started explaining the purpose of the position, its role and what it entailed. As the interviewer was speaking, I was completely lost, based on having no knowledge of the business lingo, and absolutely struggled with the language barrier and the terminology used in asking these tough questions, which I could not understand or answer. This communication breakdown left me lost for words, where English was my second language as a beginner. I was overwhelmed and failed to give an answer. Then there was a pause and, for some strange reason, something out of the ordinary flourished. The interviewer had realised I was in deep trouble. I wasn't responding and not participating in the conversation. In recognising the situation, she quickly changed the topic and switched to converse in a simpler fashion. This form of communication made it easier to interact with them. I understood how to respond and speak to exchange dialogue. This clever tactic by this woman in the heat of the moment was executed perfectly out of pure kindness. I then left on that note.

A week had passed and I had been consciously aware that I had failed miserably in every vital aspect and stood no chance of succeeding against the competition to be considered for the position. This interview had occupied my mind all week, making me feel aimless with no direction, while anticipating the phone call that bore bad news.

There was nothing I could do but wait. So, I slowly paced around, going about my usual everyday routine, while waiting for a message, in hope this would put to rest my curiosity and settle my emotions once and for all. Eventually, the call had arrived. I answered the phone to hear the decision. A woman spoke in a professional tone, stating some exciting news. She wanted to congratulate me on being a successful candidate for the temporary role within the government department. This news took me by surprise and left me speechless, as I thanked her for this opportunity.

On hearing this news, it gave me hope and boosted my confidence of feeling good, where I could partake and join the workforce in society. I couldn't explain it; this was beyond my comprehension, to be a successful candidate for a government job. No matter how you look at it, the means don't justify the ends. Was it a coincidence or divine intervention? You decide.

My time had come and I was ready to make my contribution in this world and engage in the workforce. With a willing but nervous attitude, I turned up for work. They explained to me what the role involved and the basic principle of it. This role suited me perfectly! The requirements were basic office duties that covered a wide range of areas. The simplicity of it enabled me to learn the fundamentals relating to the office environment.

During my time there, I faced many challenging tasks that were crucial to me in developing a variety of skills in the administration field. This opportunity had helped me gain more experience and understanding in the three-month period I worked there.

By then, my time had quickly passed and the term contract had reached its end date. As a result of that, the H.R. officer in charge had recognised the situation and was kind enough to meet with me and discuss my next opportunity. She took the initiative and had already recommended me for another position in the Education Department.

This was unreal and not expected by any stretch of the imagination. For obvious reasons, she must have seen potential or someone up there liked me. With all that in motion, my last day of departure had come with a farewell to the staff, and I started to look forward to the new job as promised, without delay.

Later that week, I received a phone call from the officer to arrange a time for an interview for the ongoing position in a different location. Without any hesitation, I gladly accepted this door of opportunity and eagerly waited for a chance to be part of the workforce once more.

The day was set and I planned my trip to the city to establish the foundation of the suggested organisation mentioned by the H.R. officer. I followed the instructions to the third floor and walked towards reception and stated my purpose for this visit. Lo and behold, to my amazement, I saw the same woman waiting to interview me. This same person who recommended me for the previous position was also here to meet with me on this very important occasion, in the same fashion. It seemed too good to be true; she was taking the interview.

I nervously sat down, not knowing what to do, as she began to simply point out that this meeting was just a formality and I was already the successful applicant for this position. On hearing this good news, I was overcome with joy and a sense of assurance that overcame me, despite not being qualified. This was beyond my intellectual capacity by any standard, as I would gratefully accept this gift with gladness.

Somehow things worked together for the good of my benefit, as I walked directly into the perfect role that suited my skill level. I found myself working in the registry filing and mailing room department. This multifunctional area was the engine room that helped develop my administration and social skills, to understand how things operated in the business sector and how to communicate with people in a friendly and respectful manner.

As the years passed, I became part of the furniture and had gained more experience and confidence in a gradual climb, where I began to venture out into other departments in the workplace. This opportunity would allow me to gradually learn and grow in this field.

CHAPTER 5

Time To Spread Your Wings And Fly

This new profession of working in an office environment had become an instrumental part of my life. It had enabled me to put into perspective the instinct of human desire that tends to nurture this given talent birthed within. Throughout the stages of life, it became more evident, as I established myself in the workplace, that I began to develop a sense of awareness where time passed me by in the coming age. I came to recognise there was an important piece of the puzzle missing to complete me. This feeling yearned for marriage and family, being instilled in me to satisfy the craving nature of companionship.

To accomplish this idea, I weighed up what was required and what was necessary to achieve this target; this would involve hard work and sacrifice to make it happen with the right partner. Of course, anything was possible with discipline and good planning. The first step was to identify my goal, envision my companion and start building my financial status. This effort needed a strict attitude without compromise and no distractions to reach this goal.

This plan I decided on, without fail, needed focus and determination to reach this goal. I set my sights on finding a good companion within my culture. In theory, all this sounded like a happy picture, ready to develop. All I must do was simply return to my place of origin and find the perfect mate to share my life with.

So let the mission begin. As I planned the ultimate journey, I took the necessary steps by organising travel documents and flight arrangements to coincide with times and dates. I notified my relatives overseas for my sole purpose of visiting. Everything was set and on schedule; it was just a matter of how and when to navigate this journey. Of course, it was easier said than done.

The thought of having to prepare and will myself across the ocean towards the land of hope was a tall ask, especially when I had to face those childhood memories that still lingered inside, and having to revisit those ugly memories of the past is not something you look forward to. Either way, understanding the danger of this so-called ambition was not a fool-proof idea, being well aware of the current war situation, which was unstable and unpredictable in law and order. The complete opposite to Australia, that upholds the constitution and is built on democracy. There is always an element of danger when you're under a different governance, where conflict still exists in a hostile, barren land. This type of threat causes you to be cautious and on guard, as you shift your mindset from the ordinary standard of life to a more serious location. Not an ideal situation to be playing matchmaker in another world across the ocean.

After being absent for twenty years, I didn't know what to expect. I was most likely to stumble in a social gathering, where my new beliefs were now conditioned to function in a different way that helped me embrace a sense of freedom in Western society.

This complex journey of having to revisit my relatives, where once a child, now an adult, brought a challenge in having to confront this civilisation, being a torn nation. You can only imagine the impact it could have on someone emotionally and relationally. After gaining knowledge in a modern developing world, regardless of circumstance, I was still determined to achieve this grand plan.

And so history was about to be written, as I departed on this long, daunting journey, with a sense of anticipation as to what unfolds, being carried away over the ocean shore to the land of misfortune. The land that left its mark on a torn family, which now returns a brave one in his rightful age to rewrite a new chapter that would ascribe his story when dwelling among the citizens of the place of origin. One can pursue a companion for his own delight with a similar background and fly away into the morning sun to shine his heart, while watching the clouds roll away. For the plane to break into the atmosphere of silence, while looking into the horizon that stirs your emotions with a sense of excitement.

As the plane landed at Beirut airport, I made my way out and aimed for the luggage area to claim my belongings. Once I was organised, I began to walk towards the exit gate and intently look around for a welcoming committee. There in the distance, I saw my relatives waving ecstatically and calling out for me to come over. I immediately recognised my uncles in this beautiful, engaging historical moment, that was mixed with joy and sorrow. Hearing their voices melted my heart. With open arms they began to shower me with love. This was a special moment, a memorable occasion set in time to reunite the long-awaited family member in the lost years, where the affection didn't hold back the tears of joy. Delighted by my appearance, however, it triggered the heartbreak and sad memories caused by a tragedy which forced a crucial departure in a country which produced no winners, only victims of war.

On the bright side, for my relatives these were happy days, to unite with a son of heritage, to come together and share our affairs in what had shaped and birthed our current situation in a distant land. The meet-and-greet introduction had grown by the hour, as I slowly familiarised myself with the relations for the first time.

After the introductions settled, the opportunity arose to do what was important, exploring and familiarising myself with the surroundings, to become more accustomed to this different environment, with its poverty and daily living. It needed no explanation when witnessed firsthand, as I observed the scenery in its current state and turmoil left in ruins. I wandered about with a sad look of disappointment for the onlooker to see. This turned one's attitude to admiration for the people's persistence under the circumstances that brought humility, where reality hit home, with a sincere heartfelt affection for the standard of living.

This country of demise is still surviving after all the tragedy and, despite its downfall, people are still going about their own business, regardless of the outcome. This observation brought reassurance and the possibility to connect with the right person. The potential to meet the one, with the help of my relatives who were on board with the idea and perfectly aware of my intentions and purpose of this trip. They were all in favour and very excited to be a part of this memorable event, to give away a nephew that would reproduce the family tree.

Without delay, we were ready and in agreement to explore the possibilities and begin this search on this marriage path for a suitable bride. My uncle's general idea was to simply arrange meetings with families that offered a potential and worthy partner. In doing so, they organised timely visits to get together and enjoy homely chats over coffee.

When the appropriate time came for the opportunity to present itself, my uncles spoke to the desired family and made their reason known for this special occasion. They openly expressed their intentions to the family regarding a respectable marriage with their daughter. They asked the parents in return what their ambitions towards their daughter's prospects were in relation to marriage, respectfully seeking their opinion on the matter. If a connection was made for the matter to progress further, then nature would take its course.

The arrangement of going back and forth in dialogue also had some conditions attached to it. It required both single parties to be involved in the proposal based on our expectations during this experience. This search involved many trials and errors, with no guarantee or reward for effort. I had to go with the flow. I cast my lure and waited for the right catch.

While connecting and exploring many places with all kinds of people, it wasn't long before my eyes were opened to witnessing the good, bad and broken. You quickly learn everyone has a story to tell and it spoke volumes in the areas of loss, hardship and disappointment one has to endure. When you see this kind of courage, they certainly deserve credit for their willpower and survival skills through it all.

But there also lies another kind, who love to play with evil, cleverly disguising themselves on the surface to show good intentions and make neighbourly gestures of special invites to lure their prey, and walk around with a black heart, as they cunningly plan and plot their hidden agenda that lay behind their evil deeds to gain access and win their target over.

In this case, the unfortunate turns out to be me, for I became the target of a self-seeking and well-known evil woman. She just happened to live in the same building as my relatives, where I was residing for a short time. The mother of the daughter was determined to lure me with her devious plan to capture and entice me for her daughter. "Come to my web," said the spider to the fly.

She began to weave her web by using her clever advances and subtle approach. She invited herself over to the above apartment and would show special interest in me. She was very friendly and pretended to be nice, by bringing tasty treats and putting on an act. She used it as leverage to invite her victim: "You must come for a visit to my nest of charms." This scene was repeated several times with the aim to draw me in and wear me down with her tempting offers. I was not aware of her scheme and it didn't register with me at the time. The plans she conjured up for my capture had been called upon to entice me while the trap was being set up.

In my naivety, I had no idea what was in store for me when I accepted her invitation that seemed harmless in its nature. I discovered her intentions were to get me acquainted with her daughter, who, being the pawn or the object for sale, aimed to join us together in matrimony. At the time, I didn't consider the possibility or what the intention was of this casual visit.

Perceptions can be disguised and the truth masked. I couldn't resist and found myself going back for more, as though being pulled by a force that drew me in for a close encounter for intimacy. Birthing a feeling of interest in pursuit of this person, the visits became crucial on my part, hoping to see her more often. I was spellbound and couldn't help being infatuated by her company. Somehow this superficial involvement began to take shape, causing a deeper influential connection that overrode my emotions and had formed a need to see her. This commitment had become very serious on my behalf, as I found myself desperately involved with this person, as it reached a stage where a proposal was in order.

This relationship had trouble written all over it, as gossip and the bearer of bad news travelled quickly in a small town. Naturally, this troubling news had reached my uncles, who, being my guardians and support, heard enough to bring judgment on this situation. They quickly came to my rescue and voiced their opinion on this ridiculous matter. They were in disgust and outraged by this appalling union that had taken place, having been their responsibility to look out for my interest. They strongly warned me not to get involved with these immoral people.

They were a family with a long history of evil practices that left their mark on people over a period of time. I was not aware of this, so the message was basically loud and clear: go and stop this foolish behaviour and get the idea out of your head. Furthermore, do not pursue this disgraceful act any longer or it could lead to serious ramifications on the family.

This serious talk had resonated with me and had arrested my attention. I was obligated to my uncles, who, out of deep concern, made the effort to put this fire out I had kindled. It was a reasonable request to resign from this harmful obsession I was entangled in and had little support. I understood what it meant to follow through with their request, even though I didn't like it. From my point of view, it only complicated and confused my stay. This family altercation left me in a mess of where to go next, by losing my sense of reality and direction.

I was in limbo, not knowing how to deal with this situation after hearing the bad news that marriage was forbidden in any case. So, instead of responding to my uncles' wise counsel and taking it onboard, I withdrew myself by doing the opposite and rebelling against their advice. I didn't want to end this relationship because, as strange as it seemed, I couldn't shake off the desire of wanting this even more. As if something stronger was tugging at me to continue this false companionship that had no moral basis for continuation.

I was in two minds and lost, not sure of anything that would make sense. Left to ponder this rejection, the struggle was manifesting even more. Walking around exploring the city, showing signs of not being myself, I became more evident in feeling downcast and depressed, with unstoppable negative thoughts running around my head. I'd fallen under some kind of trance or influence, where my behaviour became abnormal and noticeable, distorting my decision-making process.

Things took a toll on me and became too much to bear, finding it hard to keep company with my uncles. We couldn't reach a resolution to solve this matter. Being from two different worlds, we couldn't see eye to eye on anything. Nothing was going to change their mind; their terms were simple and final. If I rejected their help and counsel, they would wash their hands of the whole matter and leave me to my own devices. This would put a division between us and the happy journey would become sorrowful. It would lose its desires that promised a happy ending.

Now time had been wasted as things didn't go according to plan and, by that token, there was nothing more for me to say or do. In response, I saw out my remaining days by staying right away from all this commotion and moved out to live with different relatives who were based in the village, before I flew back home.

However, analysing this vain attempt was a failure from the beginning. It eventually lost control and hit a roadblock, coming to a dead end. It was pointless to persist with or escalate the problem any further, best to let go and exercise patience where I could resume normal function to some degree.

I tried to enjoy my remaining days without the hassle of dealing with the pressure. This well-deserved escape brought some balance back and gave me a sense of relief. Mingling with these wonderful relatives that occupied the village in a welcoming community, they were accommodating and hospitable with their generosity. This experience was an eye-opener in watching how the simple lived and kept their traditions. This community lived and shared common interests in one another. That inspiration gave me a new perspective on life, as I experienced it firsthand and got a glimpse of how Mum's generation lived in the agricultural life, day by day. I felt at home with the genuine love that was bestowed upon me. My stay came to an end and I headed back to Australia. I said my goodbyes and flew out of the country.

Loaded down and carrying emotional baggage back with me from this trip, it had so many twists and turns. It left me wondering, with the memories that were engraved in my mind, the regret of not securing a potential prospect in the process. It left me feeling empty-handed as I approached my destination.

Besides all that, the main objective was to come home safe and sound to a normal environment with a familiar setting. A place of comfort and assurance where I could find composure in these trying times, having been stretched beyond my capability in this battle of fight and retreat, that caused a defeating blow.

Home sweet home—the sound of freedom, my sanctuary, where I longed to recover from a tired and weary road of misfortune. I had hoped to find peace and a better life in this venture, but it did not work in my favour.

But it was not over yet, as I returned to my normal routine, time allowed me to reset and organise a second trip. Planning to reclaim the daughter of the evil mother, who for some reason caused me to feel a gravitational pull towards her. It was as though some driving force was controlling the whole situation. I was caught up in this family affair with determination to follow through with it, at any cost, to fully commit myself to saving a portion of my income again, to meet the deadline and correspond with the date.

Going back alone wouldn't do me justice; I would fail miserably at every turn. I would need to bring someone who had a greater understanding of the family's history, who could argue my case and defend me in this trial. This time I wasn't going empty-handed, but bringing the heavy artillery, being my mother, to combat this battle with my uncles, taking responsibility and giving her consent, where they could come to an agreement and give their blessings towards this marriage proposal.

This trip for Mum meant a great deal to her, in wanting to return to her homeland. This delightful news had birthed excitement in her footsteps, longing to see the relatives again after twenty years, where the scars left a heavy burden to bear. To see family and friends again meant the world to her, for an occasion such as this brought joy and closure to her heart.

At the same time, keeping in mind that this travel was more official than the previous and contained a significant amount of responsibility and diligence to put into action, I had to plan the necessary requirements that would align the travel period with our overseas relatives to accompany us to the airport.

So, when the time had arrived to fly out, preparations were in order for departure to visit homeland once more. We wished our brothers and sisters farewell and headed out for another chapter to be written in this all-consuming border crisis in the land of misfortune. After a few days had passed, we reached our destination point and landed safely in Beirut. This time the gathering had captured an audience who were anxious to see Mum, eagerly awaiting to get together with excitement.

As soon as we came in sight, something had changed in the atmosphere regarding the encounter between Mum and them, that erupted with a holler, creating a dramatic emotional scene of joy. The expressions of welcoming tears of joy in seeing one another, running with open arms of celebration, expressing a genuine love that spoke a multitude of happiness in reuniting. This was a treasured moment of finally coming together, as the cries expressed the painful loss that stirred up those suppressed emotions built inside in a war-torn country that caused a heartbreak of separation.

The luggage was sorted and we finally drove out to meet up at uncle's place of rest from this weary trip. There the conversations began to flow back and forth in harmony, being brought up to speed with the family affairs. Watching them in discussion, I could see Mum feeling a sense of relief on this blessed trip by connecting with relatives, which had been long overdue. Plenty of questions were poured out from the heart which reflected the face of disappointment and loss that spoke of the past and present. Time didn't heal all wounds in this emotional stir.

This family union cleared the air, where it mattered most, and gave the opportunity to settle and mend the heart. For we also had business to attend to and time was a factor concerning this important visit. With all due respect and in a timely manner, we allowed the week to calm down, and to not overcommit but gently revisit the missed marriage opportunity that occurred last year. This situation had caused a breakdown in communication that left us in a serious dilemma and now we could focus on this important issue.

The moment of truth had arrived for this conversation to commence. We calmly gathered together to discuss this vital issue that caused quite a stir among family members regarding the marriage of the obedient daughter in question, that had been denied the right to matrimony.

When the topic was brought to their attention, you could feel the tension in the room slowly brewing to a high temperature. This engagement had burst the gates open, as everyone wanted to give their opinion on this wrongful idea of being betrothed into an immoral family, by name and nature. This topic had the markings of war and peace, but however you tilted the scale of wrong and right, Mum had the final authority on this ruling that decided the fate of her son's happiness, no matter what the outcome prevailed. Ultimately, it was my decision to choose the desired partner, regardless of their reputation or feuds in the past.

After hearing that, it left a bad taste in their mouth and didn't go well with them. In reply, they expressed their concerns and would not give their consent and warned us not to get involved with this toxic family who had a long history of bad news, which Mum was aware of.

Of course, there was a lot of truth in their argument and every case deserved a fair trial, especially when you weighed it up and examined the facts and nature of this intermarriage. It had no cohesion to apply the principle of leave and cleave; it represented no urgency or rash decision to make it happen. So, out of respect and goodwill, it was best to give this situation time and so we left it alone for a while and allowed nature to take its course.

This observation was important because of its implication. It needed maturity to step back and disconnect from this problem. So, the best solution was to separate ourselves from this emotional involvement concerning everyone involved and refrain from any contact with the girl.

We took a break and moved away from this place. This idea gave us a cooling period to determine where the situation stood and if it was meant to be. The plan was to head towards the village and live with other relatives there. This reprieve would allow us to think more clearly and calm things down. In doing that, it relieved us from the pressure and tension this situation caused.

We were ready to take a car trip to meet those beautiful relatives of ours, but on that day suddenly something strange had happened. Incredibly, somehow a familiar person had shown up out of nowhere, that caused us to cancel our original trip and convince us to accompany him elsewhere. This bizarre timing was a mystery, how our paths had crossed. Being from the other side of the world, this person Alex, being an Australian friend, also happened to be visiting the country and had found us by chance in this part of the world.

This encounter made Mum glad, where she casually opened up and shared the whole drama that took place and the reason for the exit. Upon hearing this predicament, he persuaded us to come and stay with his relatives, who were in a distant town.

Mum had accepted his proposal to accompany him as his special guests. He offered us rooms and to board with his family friends. This sounded like a good idea somewhat, even though I was still not comfortable with this suggestion, by staying with complete strangers. I struggled with trust, in my emotional condition and fragile state, feeling discouraged in nowhere land, carrying a load I couldn't shake off. Caught up in this predicament, I didn't have a say to oppose this idea, just to follow Mum and go along pretending I'm okay.

And so a new chapter began, as we travelled a few hours to reach this residential town. It consisted of a rare kind of people who resided in this part of the country. It was open temptation, so we needed always to be on our guard from the looks of these people. We made our way to their house, where the welcoming party seemed hospitable with their grand gestures.

Our friend Alex also brought his son along, who spoke fluent English and was around my age. This connection gave me an advantage in socialising and roaming the town, wanting to explore the marketplace together.

A few days went by where the mingling and entertaining with the household members would get together to establish a connection. Alex would also take us out for some enjoyment. The house owners had two daughters; the older one would gladly join the outdoor activity. This started to generate a popularity gathering for the young adults that was building relational momentum.

The socialising gradually developed a chemistry between two people, totally unexpected. The outings had opened new possibilities, inviting the idea of a new prospect in the making. The older daughter and I took a liking to each other. This attraction had blossomed into a closer personal interaction, ready to flourish into something more serious between us. This was evident to proceed to the next level, but before we could take it any further, the proper order of courtship to relationship was to politely ask her father's permission.

So, Alex and Mum agreed to confront the father of the bride. They created a careful and tactical plan to present this idea, which was of a sensitive nature, to the father. Without hesitation, Alex, being the respectful guardian, was nominated the chief speaker and Mum negotiated the terms.

Timing was of the essence to discuss this hot topic with the father. They needed to approach with care in presenting this matter before him and hopefully have an open discussion between two parties.

The hour had come, where Alex would begin to address the topic regarding the idea of marriage relating to his daughter. But when the father heard this surprising news, he suddenly became enraged and his demeanour completely changed and transformed before us. He found this proposal outrageous and it did not go well for him. He harshly dismissed the notion and forbade any such talk regarding his daughter.

After that horror show, we saw a mean side that turned on us without explanation or reason for his disapproval. So, Alex, feeling responsible for his rude reaction and terrible manner displayed in that fashion, insisted on trying again for the sake of us. The father would not listen, only repeated his action of outburst and began avoiding us.

This picture was clearly tainted in gloom, which portrayed adversity. As a result, the matter was closed and it was pointless to push it any further.

So, plan B was put into effect. One man against an army cannot stand nor command us to retreat. And whatever reason for his madness could not easily be dismissed or forgotten due to his stubbornness. In any case, we were determined to make this work on our terms and find a way to outsmart him at this game and play by different rules. The clan planned to meet secretly and quietly on top of a building roof, with the people in favour of making this formal ceremony to join us together and confirm this bond to be official.

Shortly after that, we bowed out and quietly left the town, to go back to the main village with our relatives, who lived a simple life and opened their homes to us.

The country life there was relaxing and I certainly could not complain about the friendships and the wonderful variety of food we enjoyed eating. Unfortunately, our remaining days were getting shorter, in keeping with our flight schedule.

On the last day, we were transported to the airport, said our sad goodbyes with God's blessing of farewell. The plane was on the way to Melbourne Airport, which was a welcoming sigh of relief, to be back to normal civilisation.

This didn't leave much room for happiness, where a second journey did not work out in the area of marriage that did not guarantee a common companion for me. But not everyone goes through this trouble and distress and becomes a carrier of misfortune. More like an offbeat instrument, as I paced around carrying those disturbing experiences that complicated my entire life and lay in waste and ruin.

I tried to comprehend this cruel and selfish act that served no peace or goodwill toward fellow men. This outcome gave no real indication for a future prospect. It only left me to take on a whole new role of responsibility, which added a whole new dimension to this engagement.

This inner struggle of being oceans apart took a toll on me, to somehow keep in touch by phone to hear any progress that would produce a reality in these promised vows.

As the days and months faded by, losing touch, I could only entertain the idea as the signs became more evident that I was losing ground and time was slowly drifting us apart. It was hard to continue a distant relationship with so many obstacles in the way. Eventually, common sense prevailed and I let go. This one-sided relationship cost me a lot of time and became a setback instead of a setup in trying to build something out of nothing. I came to terms with this out-of-reach pursuit and decided enough time had been wasted. It was best for me to focus on more important and worthwhile things, like working alongside my immediate family and planning our futures.

From now on, it was business as usual for me, where structure and stability would come into order. Even then, you still remember the casualties after the effect of a major event that took place. Along the way, I collected numerous hardships that tarnished my soul. Even though I was in a much better place, yet still something kept bothering me in reaching my full potential, to function properly.

The signs were obvious and convincing, as the wheel of failure and disappointment started winding in motion. I struggled to succeed at various things in the natural realm of ordinary. This mystery that mirrored a deeper sense of emotional distress had developed a pattern of defeat in this inner battle of tug-of-war, constantly at work to pull me down and cause a shift into the unknown.

Occurring situations would systemically bring confusion in the mind, by repeatedly confessing the negative side of things in a simple situation. This unfamiliar encounter continued to pursue and evolve in me on every occasion, ready to display its evil side and create this victim mentality behaviour.

CHAPTER 6

What The Heck

A year had now passed, and nothing had developed in this relationship. Out of curiosity, I kept in contact with her overseas, but to no avail. This prospect began to fade, and reality proved itself for distant hearts. What once seemed full of possibility gradually lost its sense of adventure. As a result, I lowered my expectations, realising this was not meant to be. Still, I was grateful for the efforts of Alex and the others who had gone to great lengths to try to make it work on that rooftop.

Everything in my life seemed to slow down, and the wasted time took its toll on me. I ended up carrying a heavy burden, and my heart grew weary, needing to be refreshed.

There was no point in refusing to move on. It was better to resume my normal habits and return to a lifestyle that would help me mentally and emotionally, allowing one door to close so another could open. The damage had been done, and there would be no compensation or justice for the one who had lost. There was no point in seeking revenge. The matter was closed.

The routine of work, play and rest began to rebuild momentum in my daily life. I started to let go of the old relationship, allowing it to slowly fade away and trusting that time would calm things down—or so I thought.

Then, on a certain day, something unexpected arrived and brought a sudden change in the wind of my life. A letter came for me from my country of origin.

When I returned home from work, I was told that a letter from overseas had arrived, addressed to me personally. I was surprised and unsure how to react. I could not understand why such a letter would come from someone I had already given up on. As far as I knew, there had been no attempt to rekindle this long-dead relationship. I felt reluctant to even know what was inside. Still, out of curiosity, I asked a family member to read it aloud.

As the letter was read, its contents did not sound convincing. It did not feel genuine, and the words made little sense to me. There was an apology of sorts, mixed with regret, saying that it was better this way—that everything should end, and goodbye. This left me puzzled, because from my point of view, the matter had already ended. I had no intention of pursuing the relationship any further. So why had this letter come now?

What happened next felt like an extraordinary act of evil. The story, it seemed, was far from over. I was about to enter a whole new world—one that felt like a horror show. That same night, something unwelcome seemed to come with that letter, as though evil itself had been sealed inside it. What I experienced was unthinkable and completely unknown to me. This supernatural attack would affect my life on a whole new level. It left me in a state of terror and shock. Whatever had attached itself to that letter was ready to pounce on me while I slept.

As I lay sleeping, an invisible force suddenly came over my body. I felt a powerful surge shake me violently and uncontrollably in bed. In fear and shock, I began to scream as the torment intensified. This dark force was beyond my strength or ability to resist. I was powerless against it.

Lying there helpless, overwhelmed by what felt like a spiritual attack, I sensed a heavy darkness cast over me that would not let go. This strange and disturbing force seemed to push itself upon me, entering deeply into my being and taking hold without resistance.

This was the beginning of many terrifying nights that changed my life and led me into confusion. I could feel this evil presence taking hold of me and affecting every part of my being. It left me helpless and powerless. Whatever this was, it began to play a major role in my life, trapping and confining me as though I were in a small prison cell of torment.

As a result of this strange incident, which happened without warning, the news spread quickly among those who wanted to know about it. People were drawn in to witness it and offer their opinions. It defied logic, yet regardless of what anyone believed, I was the one living through it—the victim of something I could not understand, battling what felt like an enemy of my soul and desperately needing freedom.

Questions arose for an ordinary man: what did all this mean? Fear had filled my heart. Who would take pity on me? Who would help me in my pain and lead me out of it? I was filled with anguish by this affliction that had brought my life to a halt and placed me in an impossible situation.

Because of this distress, my search for help became a desperate quest for freedom. I needed answers. I needed some explanation for what was happening to me. I longed to undo this work of darkness and find relief from the grip of this enemy that seemed to hold me captive day and night. Evening itself became something I dreaded.

This darkness would torment me night after night, causing my body to shake and tremble in terror. The experience became like clockwork. It robbed me of sleep, affected my mental health and wellbeing, and began to show in the rhythm of my daily life.

CHAPTER 7
Identity Crisis

Through this overwhelming experience, I came to understand that there are things in life we simply cannot control. This truth became clear when I was confronted with its reality. Not everything works itself out. Things do not automatically get better on their own—this belief is a myth.

Speaking from experience, I have learned that life is not always fair and often carries many troubles. This reality hits home when you are faced with the truth. Every day is not sunshine and roses. Either way, time does not stop, or the ocean cares when you're drowning. You find yourself hoping for something to rescue you from adversity, but when you are in a hole, all you can do is look up.

In these unusual trials, I can testify to how life can suddenly catch you off guard when you least expect it, striking you with a crushing blow.

Life can throw all kinds of unexpected challenges at you—things that affect your emotions and your heart. These problems can create a ripple effect that overwhelms you completely. Having to deal with such a critical situation can change everything. It is remarkable how quickly things can shift. One day, life is steady; the next, your world is turned upside down. It only takes one terrible incident to transform your life—from good to bad, and from bad to worse—until everything seems to come crashing down.

Imagine if someone could have foretold your life, describing it as filled with unimaginable trouble. It would be difficult to comprehend such a future. We are limited in our ability to see ahead. We are bound by time, unable to fully understand our purpose or what lies before us. This limitation reminds us of the need for a greater perspective—one that only God can provide. Yet we live in a fallen world that often rejects its Creator and embraces darkness instead.

Things can go wrong at any stage of life. A single unexpected event can leave a deep emotional scar that carries through time. This kind of damage can push a person into fear and hopelessness. It can even cause someone to create a false image of themselves as a way to cope—a shield to protect against the pain and to provide a sense of security.

These hidden scars are all too familiar for those who have experienced deep hurt. Beneath the surface lie wounds formed through life's devastating moments—when everything shifts from normal to something completely different.

I came to realise that what I was facing was not just natural, but spiritual. It was something far beyond my ability to fight. All I had was a religious Catholic background, which had not equipped me with an understanding of this kind of struggle. I had little knowledge of the Bible and no real foundation in these matters. The tools I had were ineffective against what I was facing.

So I began searching for answers. I gathered whatever information I could, hoping someone would guide me to the right help. I turned towards spiritual leaders, looking for direction. My goal was simple—I was desperate and willing to receive anything that might help.

This condition took precedence over everything else in my life. I became consumed with finding a way to overcome it, regardless of the cost. I was determined to be free.

I reached out to religious believers who were known to deal with these kinds of issues. My purpose was clear—I needed this thing gone.

CHAPTER 8

Trial & Error & What May Come

I was ready and willing, even though I was still uncertain about what lay ahead or what to expect. One thing was certain—I was being tormented at every turn by this invisible force that had no intention of leaving. Month after month, it proved itself relentless. Desperate times called for desperate measures.

So I began searching for help—someone who could guide me towards restoration. This led me to my first connection: a Catholic priest, recommended to me. I gathered the courage to visit a church and speak with him. When the opportunity came, I explained my unusual situation. I shared how I felt overwhelmed and unwell, affected by this ongoing spiritual disturbance.

In response, he sympathised but suggested it was likely stress. He whispered a few words over me and then left. He offered no real answers, no direction—nothing helpful. It was a disappointing encounter. Clothed in priestly garments, yet seemingly unequipped to deal with the reality of what I was facing.

Still, this was a learning experience. I refused to let one setback stop my search. I chose to remain positive and continue looking for the next person who might help.

So where would I find the answer? Was it hidden somewhere unknown? Time and opportunity often reveal what we seek. Through word of mouth, some friends heard about my struggle and recommended a Greek Orthodox priest.

With nothing to lose, we went to the church and waited patiently. Eventually, he approached us. I shared my story through my Greek-speaking friends. But before anything meaningful could happen, he simply stood up and walked away—without a word. No questions. No response. Nothing.

We were left stunned.

This second disappointment hit hard. I had expected compassion, or at least some guidance. Instead, I encountered indifference. It became clear to me that many of these religious leaders had no understanding of the spiritual realm I was dealing with. This troubled me deeply.

So I widened my search. I needed someone equipped—someone who could actually confront what I was facing. My condition was worsening. It was affecting my wellbeing, and I knew this was not simply a medical or mental issue. It required something beyond the natural.

Through friends, I was introduced to a Coptic priest who was said to understand these matters more deeply. This sounded promising.

When we met, he was different. He listened. He took me seriously. He didn't dismiss me or treat me like I was imagining things. Instead, he engaged with me and began helping me process what I was experiencing. This gave me hope.

We began a series of sessions.

The deliverance took place in a quiet room at the church. He read prayers from a religious text while I sat in anticipation. Soon, my body began to react—shaking and stirring, as if something inside me had been awakened.

Seeing this, the priest began commanding whatever was inside me to leave. He spoke with authority, repeating his commands. I trembled and cried out, but nothing changed. There was no release.

We tried again over several sessions. Despite our efforts, the result was the same. Nothing shifted.

Although we didn't succeed, I appreciated his willingness to help. At least he acknowledged the reality of what I was facing.

Meanwhile, my condition worsened. The exhaustion showed on my face. Nights became unbearable. Sleep was almost impossible. I was desperate just to function.

Eventually, I turned to a doctor for temporary relief. I explained my sleep issues and was prescribed sleeping tablets—just to get through the nights.

Not long after, another opportunity arose. We were introduced to a man who practised spiritual healing using his own methods. Desperate, I agreed to see him.

He wrote something on paper, folded it into a triangular shape, and sealed it. He instructed me to wear it around my neck at all times. Then he placed an old ritual book on my chest.

Suddenly, I felt a release—a sensation as though something had left me.

For a moment, I was hopeful.

But it didn't last.

The next day, everything returned—worse than before.

This was the beginning of a pattern.

We sought out others—men who practised similar rituals. One charged us money and promised results. Nothing happened. Another performed similar actions. Again, no change.

Each attempt left me more discouraged.

Then one night, things escalated.

While lying on the floor beside a friend, I began seeing figures moving around the room. I could feel them—like something was wrestling and passing through me. It was terrifying.

I couldn't understand what was happening.

By this point, my perspective had shifted. Fear and confusion began to dominate my thinking. I became desperate—willing to try anything to be free.

Even if it meant stepping outside my own beliefs.

Some of my friends were Muslim, and through them I was introduced to someone who specialised in Islamic exorcism. Despite the difference in faith, I agreed. I just wanted freedom.

Before the process began, I was asked to recite a prayer and formally accept Islam. In my desperation, I agreed.

Almost immediately after, I felt something unusual enter me.

Then the session began.

I was taken into a dark room and told to lie on the floor between two speakers playing Islamic prayers. After some time, a man suddenly approached me, grabbed me, shouted aggressively, and began slapping me—commanding the spirit to leave.

I was completely shocked.

Then came a second method—he began striking my feet with a stick.

Still, nothing changed.

Instead, I was left physically and emotionally shaken.

They tried again—this time at my home. The same methods were repeated, but more aggressively. Finally, they brought out a power cord with exposed wires.

When they applied it, I felt an intense electric shock surge through my body. The pain was unbearable.

At that moment, my sister intervened.

Seeing what was happening, she stepped in and forced them out, furious at their dangerous actions. She likely saved my life.

After they left, I slowly recovered. But the damage—physically and mentally—was significant.

This experience left me with more questions than answers.

How could these methods possibly defeat something unseen? How could such brutality be considered a solution?

What I encountered was not help—it was harm.

And still… I remained trapped.

CHAPTER 9

SOS Is Anybody Out There

At this point, confusion in my life had taken a complete turn, and my friendships and lifestyle began to reflect a very different social image. The normal elements of life no longer followed a natural pattern. This affliction had undone the ordinary routine that had once been established in my nature and personality. After all these trials and tribulations—which had resulted in financial loss and ongoing turmoil—it is no surprise that I became disheartened and discouraged by this endless series of disappointments. In my soul-searching and cry for help, I had confronted false religious representations and ungodly characters who drew from the wrong source, only adding more spiritual carnage to my life.

Becoming so deeply involved in all these religious experiences only increased the problem and brought no comfort. I decided to stop chasing spiritual gurus for healing and answers. My expectations had dropped dramatically, as I had watched these people operate from natural thinking, adopting traditions and ideologies that failed on every account. When tried and tested, they proved powerless and only led people further astray into bondage of soul. It was time to stop, otherwise the cycle would never end.

After so many attempts, it had taken a great toll on me and left a hollow impression. Because of these experiments, I was heading towards a breakdown. Depression and low self-esteem made the journey difficult, and though I tried to hide it, the sadness on my face was turning my cheer into gloom.

This new life of misfortune created in me a sense of surrender as the months rolled by. A dark cloud seemed to hang over my head, and I could not escape the adversity that carried the memories of bitter loss and the sting of death. This battle with darkness continued to linger, bringing only discomfort and torment that multiplied in my search for freedom. At my lowest point, I felt as though I were trapped in a deep pit, crying out to be pulled out and cleansed from the ashes that stained my soul. In the midst of that pain, my spirit longed to be satisfied by a Redeemer, in the presence of His love.

For a long time, this cry for surrender and salvation had lain deep within my heart. There was a vacuum that needed to be filled—a tiny flame that needed to be fanned into fire. This quiet cry within me was always longing to connect with its Maker. My soul yearned to be free from the lies that had stolen the joy of life and replaced it with a false narrative. Blinded by glitter that did not reflect its true colours, I had walked a long road of uncertainty. This mountain climb became overwhelming, leaving me staring into the horizon for hope, trying to keep my balance and avoid falling deeper into darkness.

Giving up was not in my nature. I was determined not to collapse or fold, but to press through this unbearable pain that distorted my vision and brought me to the edge of death. What I was experiencing was not an illusion or some form of mental instability. I was fully aware of its reality. It was not something I could negotiate with or simply dismiss. To settle for defeat was not an option. I remained committed to striving for hope within the limits of my humanity and through this chain of events.

Persistence would not let me cave in. I kept fighting. My will to survive would not allow me to surrender to such torment. Even without any dramatic visitation or obvious help to spur me on, I kept believing that it was not over.

There was still an internal cry within me, and my trust in God had not disappeared. On the contrary, it was my weak faith that needed light, truth and evidence to grow stronger. If that was to happen, I needed to make changes. I needed to point my compass in the right direction in my pursuit of happiness, seeking the true God and a better source of healing. When one door closes, another opens.

So I chose a new path—one that would involve a more peaceful connection. I made it my aim to wait for a better opportunity. By this stage, my condition was no longer a secret. People widely knew what I was going through. It also meant I had reached a conclusion: I would reject anything associated with false religion. It had already caused enough damage. From that point on, my interest was purely in Christianity.

Without hesitation, my wonderful auntie recommended a lively local Christian church near her home. On hearing this, I decided to attend one of their regular services, and I thoroughly enjoyed it. I found it pleasant, comforting and full of life in its charismatic expression. At the end of the service, two kind elderly men approached me, happy to share the love of God.

During our conversation, they offered to pray for me, and I gladly accepted. As they prayed, I felt a warm sensation of relief come over me. I was surprised by its effect. They used no physical force—only words of love and faith. This prayer touched something deep within me. It awakened a longing and pointed me towards something greater. It was as though I had discovered a hidden treasure. This encounter gave me hope and stirred something in my heart to move towards this kind of love.

Unfortunately, the feeling did not last long. When night came, the darkness tormented me again. But this prayer had done something new in me. It had touched my heart and pointed me in the right direction.

On another occasion, a kind friend shared with me information about a particular group of Christians who dealt with this kind of spiritual activity. As soon as I heard this, something within me leapt. I knew I needed to respond.

Without delay, I contacted the minister and shared my story openly and sincerely, pouring out the cry of my heart. In response, he was not shaken or frightened by what I told him. He did not retreat. Instead, he welcomed the conversation with faith and confidence, like a warrior unafraid of the battle. We arranged to meet so that he could better understand the situation. What struck me most was the authority and confidence with which he spoke. It awakened in me a fresh sense of expectation. I wondered what kind of power would be used to confront this darkness.

When the day arrived, three people came to visit me. After brief introductions, they began asking me questions about my faith and my situation. This opened the door for them to share the Bible with me. They explained who Jesus was and why He had died on the cross—that His purpose was to destroy sin and evil. This good news sat deeply and rightly within me. I had no objection at all. In fact, I wanted to know more and was drawn to this beautiful faith. There was something genuine and different about them. You could feel the love and peace in their presence. I sensed no hidden agenda, no false motive—only care and sincerity.

As they shared the message of the Cross, I gladly accepted their invitation to receive Jesus Christ as my Lord and Saviour. They asked me to repeat after them in a prayer of repentance and forgiveness of sin. As I did, I felt reconnected to God, as though something broken had been restored.

My heart was overwhelmed with a deep sense of belonging and a love without boundaries.

Then they laid hands on me and began to pray in Jesus' name with power and authority, commanding all evil to leave me. In that very moment, I was overwhelmed by a sensation of love and joy. Instantly, I felt cleansed and purified from all evil, and I was astonished by the transformation. I was overflowing with the tangible presence of God and the wonder of His love. It was real. I had found a treasure beyond anything I had known.

This encounter satisfied every part of my being. It filled the empty void inside me and answered the deep hunger I had carried for so long. All my life there had been a yearning in me, a longing for something missing to make me whole. In that moment, it felt as though the missing piece had finally been found.

When the prayer ended, I was overjoyed. I felt free. Life had been breathed back into me, as though heaven had touched my heart. It was like coming home. This spiritual awakening stirred my spirit and ignited in me a desire for more of this pure love. It was as though a prison door had been opened, and hope had finally entered.

This was a brand-new beginning—one that restored my soul and turned ugliness into beauty. It marked a fresh start and the beginning of a meaningful new journey. The first thing I sought was a Bible. Then I began connecting with church people and attending a Bible study group for fellowship, where we learned the principles of God. Through the Word of God, I began to understand His ways, His morals, and the peace He brings into our lives. His Word also revealed the reality of evil and the keys to finding freedom from the darkness that follows sin and curses.

This spiritual growth was an ongoing process. It brought knowledge and understanding that helped me confront what had entered my life. Through faith, hope and love—growing deeper with maturity—I began learning how to have victory. This new excitement drew me closer to God as I tasted and saw the reward of walking with Him. Eternal life, purpose, truth and freedom were now before me. I had found the antidote to my problem.

This new commitment became a great source of confidence. It stirred my soul and led me to seek a larger church where I could continue to grow and nurture the gifting and calling placed within me. Through another believer, a church was recommended to me, and so I attended my first Sunday service there. It was large, vibrant and filled with people from many cultures. The worship band played, the congregation sang, and the words appeared on a screen. It was unfamiliar to me, but I loved it. I felt comfortable and at home. As I stood there in worship, inwardly crying out to the Lord for help regarding my situation, something unusual happened.

Suddenly, I was caught up in a heavenly vision that flashed before my eyes. I saw a person holding an infant in their arms—a perfect image of a family. It caught my attention, and I cried out within myself, "Who is this, Lord?" Then it vanished.

From this experience, I understood that the Lord was showing me a sign connected to my circumstances. He had given me a glimpse of my future—a promise that touched the very longing of my heart and hinted at the answer to my loneliness. It seemed to come with an invitation: follow Him, and He would give me the desires of my heart.

This revelation, this personal encounter with the Lord, gave me a preview of something far beyond my natural understanding. It showed me that a better life was possible. Compared to all the pain and disappointment of the alternative, this was a far greater offer—love, joy, peace and eternal life. It felt like a deal made in heaven. That confirmation inspired me to commit myself to this Christian, charismatic, Spirit-filled church. I began to enjoy the services and listened intently to the message preached by the pastor.

This uplifting moment secured my future in the Lord, and I decided to become a church member—a new convert aligning my life with God's way. I wanted to learn more deeply and build my life on a solid foundation. As I observed and participated, I began to grasp more of what Christianity meant. I formed friendships with people who shared the same passion for God.

This connection grafted me back into God's family tree. Where once I had been broken off, I was now reconnected with a thankful heart, ready to bear good fruit and leave behind the chaos that had held me down.

As I walked in this new life, things slowly began to look up. The crashing waves had eased, though the internal spiritual struggle had not entirely disappeared. In the deepest waters, support came through people who prayed, ministered and encouraged me not to give up. That kind of relationship kept me strong, with God as the centre of my growth. I was deeply grateful for the salvation that pointed heavenward.

Hungry to grow spiritually, I became more involved and joined a Bible study fellowship group. This gave me the chance to interact with others, share stories and talk about daily challenges. It was all part of the process of renewing my mind and moving in the right direction—discovering the hidden treasures and mysteries of God revealed in His Word. It offered a better life than the old one ever had.

Yet the things I had accumulated over the course of my life did not instantly disappear, even though I had been cleansed from sin. These spiritual strongholds still lingered and continued to affect my decisions. The struggle still had influence over me. Crossing from darkness to light was not easy. Some of these things still manifested to a degree, and prayer would restrain them, but the battle was not fully gone. This kind of oppression required a deeper level of faith and maturity, together with the right understanding to drive out the enemy of my soul.

My conversion did not erase my past. I still carried the history, pain and oppression I had inherited. When you are weighed down by this kind of darkness, it becomes extremely difficult to manage in hard times. Things seem to accumulate from every side. In desperation, I began looking for relief from the pain of those ugly memories and the fragile heart they had produced.

Because I hated this torment so much, I chose an unhealthy escape. The pain and sadness had become so intense, and the lies so overwhelming, that I could not bear it any longer. In desperation, I took a handful of sleeping tablets, hoping they would bring comfort from the suffering I had endured. I swallowed them and quietly lay down on the couch.

I wanted the torment to stop—the constant pounding in my mind, the consuming agony. But things did not go according to plan. What I had intended came to a halt. Instead of slipping away, something greater interrupted. I found myself calling the Christian leader who had first brought me to the Lord. He was leading a home Bible study that night when I rang him and confessed what I had done.

On hearing this, he responded with compassion and immediately prayed, asking the Lord to protect me from harm. After that prayer, something changed. Strength returned to me. I felt revived and could not fall asleep.

This event could be interpreted in many ways, but to me, the greater power prevailed. It was a miracle—an interruption from heaven. It also raised deep questions: Why do bad things happen to good people? Who is behind the evil that seeks to destroy? But through it all, I came to realise that life still mattered, and that even in the midst of chaos, there was still hope.

This experience changed my outlook. It made me want to continue pursuing this relationship with God and motivated me to spend more time with believers who could help me grow and feed my soul with true spiritual nourishment.

Growing in the Lord became my main objective. I began paying closer attention to the meaning of life, shifting my focus away from myself and towards what I could do for others. I wanted to make a difference in their lives through the power of testimony. A testimony is a powerful thing when you share what God has done—how He lifts you from trouble, darkness and despair, and gives you beauty for ashes.

The good news of the gospel became a revelation to me. It opened my eyes. Every day, I learned how important it was to care about other people's stories as well as my own. This understanding lifted my spirit and gave me a more positive outlook on life. As I walked in love and agreed with God's desire for people to be saved, I found myself in good company.

You do not need a formula to speak a kind word—just a heart for the lost and a willingness to shine a little light. It has nothing to do with perfection or skill. Those are just excuses that must be overcome. Step out in faith and trust the Lord in the process. The truth is simple: you are either for Him or against Him. If you love the Lord, then you are capable of doing what pleases Him.

Of course, there are many factors involved in pleasing the Lord. A person must have the right attitude, the right environment and the right mindset in order to grow well. This was often difficult for me, because I still struggled with old spheres of influence and friendships that pulled me back and forth. These negative and troubled lifestyles dragged me down and threatened to keep me in a vicious cycle that led nowhere.

I could see where that road was heading. The old nature and its habits still tried to rise up, especially where the pleasures of sin were concerned. I was still vulnerable to the influence of ungodly people and the desire for social acceptance. At times, I was easily shaken because the truth had not yet taken deep enough root in my heart to fully produce good fruit.

I had many flaws and weaknesses that affected my decision-making. They impacted my finances, my maturity and my development into adulthood. Training and education had been limited in my earlier years. These deficiencies can have a serious effect when you are trying to establish yourself in life. If left unchecked, they can lead to heartache, regret and poor decisions.

Even so, regardless of background or upbringing, a person can still pursue their dreams with hard work and determination. My limitations did not stop me from wanting a future of my own. I longed to buy a house—a place to call home. Eventually, an opportunity arose for my immediate family to go into partnership and purchase our first property together, with the intention of later branching out into separate homes. In time, as finances and equity improved, a split arrangement was made. The property was divided three ways, and I agreed to continue managing it by taking over the mortgage.

This challenge tested my maturity. I had not grown up with a guardian or mentor to teach me how to navigate life wisely. I had no one to guide me or help me weigh up the consequences of major decisions. So I took matters into my own hands, sometimes making drastic choices without fully realising the effect they would have on my mental health. Out of loneliness and fear of failure, I ignored warning signs.

I came up with what seemed like a brilliant plan, but it was destined to cause trouble. I decided to rent out the spare rooms to boarders for extra income and companionship. I began connecting with people and looking for suitable tenants who could also become housemates.

At first, the arrangement seemed to work. The boarders appeared decent and reliable. But they did not come alone—they brought their emotional baggage, their habits and their behaviours with them.

For the first few months, it was like a honeymoon period. Then their bad manners began to show. Rules and respect meant little to them. Their disorderly conduct created strain, and their true nature gradually surfaced. For someone like me—a quiet peacemaker—it became increasingly difficult to deal with. Before long, it felt as though my home had become a halfway house where people came and went as they pleased.

My heart was troubled as I watched so many dysfunctional people indulge in affairs, pleasures and destructive behaviour. It was an eye-opening experience, revealing the condition of the human heart and the way moral disorder opens the door to victim thinking and chaos.

It became obvious that I wanted everyone out of the house sooner rather than later. I longed to separate myself from the mess and hoped that, in time, the message would become clear and they would leave.

But in the midst of all this, temptation set a trap for me. My lonely heart was drawn towards a troubled and insecure girl who shared a similar background and culture. Through a series of events, a connection formed between us, and the idea of a relationship began to grow. Yet she came with a negative circle of friends and a lifestyle shaped by substances, addictions and the pressure to fit in.

Even so, this did not stop me from continuing to walk with the Lord. In fact, she became curious and started attending our Bible study group. The discussions about right living affected her, and for a while she seemed torn between good and evil, conviction and temptation. But it did not last. Her insecurities and troubled life kept pulling her back, and eventually the back-and-forth became too much.

Our relationship reached breaking point. It was proving to be an obstacle rather than a blessing. The partnership was lopsided, marked by little commitment or responsibility. I found myself constantly putting out little fires, while she remained carefree and unstable. The reality became clear—we did not truly share the same values, and we were completely different in the areas that mattered most.

The signs were obvious. The burden was growing heavy. Trying to carry her struggles as well as my own became too much. My attempts to support and reform her gradually lost their effect. What I had invested in was not real love and devotion, but more like a fantasy that offered a poor return.

Even so, this disappointment did not destroy my resolve. I remained determined to separate myself from a morally bankrupt world and from the habits that kept inviting temptation. I was willing to become more fully part of church life and cut the unhealthy ties.

CHAPTER 10

Enduring Hardships

(The definition of the insider: an undercover agent working for the evil side.)

Once we moved past the crisis as a wavering couple with different views on life, not much really changed. On a positive note, we did continue attending the Bible study group, which was a shared interest for both of us. We wanted to learn the truth and be fed spiritually under moral direction.

On one occasion at the Bible study group, a visiting preacher was invited as a guest speaker to share her life experiences and the challenges she had faced throughout her life. Her intention was to encourage us. After she had finished speaking, we were invited to receive prayer. I found her story very interesting, especially as she spoke about her own battles. I wondered whether she might be able to offer some spiritual insight into my situation and shed light on what I was facing. The meeting, however, was not long enough to discuss my condition in any real depth. The best option was to stay connected with her by attending the Sunday service she held in a small community hall, which I began to do in my search for answers.

While attending, I noticed that one person there—*the insider*—was also part of the fellowship. He appeared mature, knowledgeable and willing to offer help with troubling issues. After the service, I would often share my struggles with him, which seemed harmless and convenient at the time. He would listen and then offer what sounded like thoughtful, comforting answers. Over time, these conversations became a habit, and we gradually formed a bond. As a result, he would visit me on certain occasions. For whatever reason, he took a particular interest in me, and being naïve, I did not notice anything unusual. I was still a young Christian and lacked the discernment to recognise what genuine faith looked like in a person.

As this friendship developed over time, he began to display some strange behaviours. At that stage, all I wanted was to understand what God was doing in my life—how He was not only concerned with delivering me, but also with developing my character. I was captivated by this mystery, which is revealed by faith as we walk in the abundant life God gives.

This new faith naturally began to change my surroundings in an orderly way, working to remove the ungodly influences that had divided my soul. It produced blessing by stripping away the old and developing a renewed nature within me. The love of God had shown me that I was valuable in His sight, helping me shake off the desires of the world and the things I had been unable to resolve.

Even the boarders staying in my house began to leave one by one, with little effort on my part, as though by God's hand. It was an incredible relief to watch the ungodly influences depart. What a wonderful moment that was. Stability and order began to return to my life after so long being consumed by other people's endless problems, to the point that I had put my own plans on hold for their sake.

Finally, I could focus again on what was important in my own life—doing the things that mattered, living in a healthier and steadier environment, and no longer feeling stagnant.

As the days turned into months, this season allowed me to re-evaluate my future. Time had come full circle, and I began to consider the possibility of providing a place of security for Mum. After giving it considerable thought, it seemed right to hand over the house to my family for Mum to live in. I felt content with the idea of renting a bungalow from an old friend who had come into my path at just the right time. This arrangement would help me build towards a new home of my own.

This exciting new season gave me the opportunity to start fresh and allow God to continue renewing me, especially after the toll of the old relationship. I had spent so much time putting out little fires, and it had caused me great heartache. What made it worse was that she seemed to create drama without regard for the consequences. Then she discovered another place of worship on one of her many restless pursuits. That kind of free-spirited lifestyle was never for me, and the message became clear. The alarm bells for total separation were sounding, and I knew I needed to cut ties. In prayer, I said, "Lord, if this is not from You, please take it away, no matter what the cost."

On one occasion, I decided to visit her to see how she was going. What I discovered astonished me. She told me the latest news in what seemed to be her imagined act of faith—God had apparently shown her who her future husband would be, and she was now engaged.

The news shocked me. I could hardly believe that, in such a short time, someone could so easily convince themselves of such an extraordinary substitute for real love. In my confused and wounded state of mind, I walked away in disgust after that performance. I quickly chose to move on, for better or worse, trusting that God would bring the right person into my life despite the hurt that still remained deep within me. My prayer became, "God, please repair the damage and salvage this wreckage from this morally bankrupt world."

As that chapter of trouble-filled romance finally closed, I was left to manage my own life and begin making necessary adjustments. I wanted to focus on my short stay in the quiet bungalow. I needed time to reset, rebuild, and begin saving a deposit towards a new place to call home. The availability of the bungalow came unexpectedly when I happened to reconnect with a friend and shared my situation with him. To my surprise, he felt strongly in his heart that I was the right person to occupy the room. It seemed clear to me that this opportunity had been orchestrated through divine intervention—a chance to begin again and wave goodbye to the old life.

This new season, laying a fresh foundation and being built on better promises, launched me into a more conservative lifestyle. It stood in sharp contrast to the old way of living and was shaped by a new nature grounded in the commandments of God. Being part of a church fellowship established a new standard of life for me. It also gave birth to a new kind of friendship and social connection. Over time, these relationships deepened and people began gathering more regularly.

Yet this new circle also included *the insider*, who would deliberately invite himself over, disguised in a way that fooled everyone while quietly setting his evil agenda in motion.

CHAPTER 11

Twist & Turn

My time living alone in the bungalow had reached two years, and the opportunity to save a deposit for a new home had finally become a reality. This exciting transition into owning a home of my own brought a real sense of achievement. It marked a significant milestone and brought me one step closer to preparing for marriage.

Once everything was approved, the home was finalised with the bank and settled with all the necessary arrangements to make it liveable. However, this familiar situation soon began to repeat itself. After establishing myself, I once again fell into financial strain trying to maintain the house.

So, as before, I reached out to bring in boarders—people within my circle of friendships—to help manage the expenses. The problem was that this decision also brought in people with their own habits, desires and self-indulgent lifestyles. It was a foolish move on my part. I soon realised that broken people often come with complex needs. They constantly needed reminding of house rules and boundaries, especially when it came to inappropriate behaviour.

Taking on this "big brother" role pushed me to my limits. Enforcing rules and maintaining order became exhausting. Trying to create a stable and respectful environment proved to be a constant challenge.

Even visitors from church contributed to the strain. Many would come and unload their personal struggles and issues onto me. Over time, this took a toll on my emotional and mental health. I became overwhelmed, slipping into a deep state of exhaustion and depression. I withdrew from people and isolated myself for a time. I struggled to function mentally and physically, and for two weeks I found myself unable to do much more than lie on the couch.

By this point, the ongoing issues with boarders had gone on long enough. For the sake of my own sanity, I finally took a stand. I told everyone to move out immediately. It was clear that I was repeating past mistakes that had already proven harmful. No matter how much I tried to maintain standards, some people resisted and even responded negatively to my expectations. But with persistence and determination, the house was eventually cleared out. Peace and order returned, bringing a much-needed sense of calm and relief.

Despite this, people from church continued to visit for fellowship. My home became a place where individuals could come together, share real-life struggles and support one another. It was a safe space where people could speak openly about personal challenges and find connection with others who understood.

This informal gathering began to grow naturally. People were drawn to the authenticity and openness of the environment. Many came simply to talk, share and find understanding. Word spread quickly, and before long, church leaders became aware of what was happening.

Recognising the need, they saw an opportunity to step in and provide structure and direction. Seeing people who were "like sheep without a shepherd," they decided to take hold of the gathering and formalise it.

Without hesitation, the home group was officially established, and regular meetings were held at my place. A variety of people attended, enjoying the relaxed and welcoming environment. Even the church leaders were surprised by the turnout—young adults especially were drawn in, looking for connection, answers and a sense of belonging.

The idea was contagious. It created a new kind of fellowship where people felt free to express themselves and relate to others in a meaningful way. However, as the group grew, the church began introducing structured programs based on its broader model for growth and expansion.

Over time, this shift began to change the atmosphere. The simplicity and authenticity that once defined the group started to fade. People gradually lost interest as the focus shifted towards systems and programs rather than genuine connection and spiritual growth. The freedom that once existed began to feel restricted. Although there was plenty of teaching and information, there was little practical help for overcoming the real spiritual battles people were facing.

During this time, *the insider* continued operating quietly in the background, pursuing his hidden agenda. His aim was to influence and entangle me, attempting to transfer his own spiritual bondage into my life.

Meanwhile, church life continued as usual. Programs were repeated, cycles continued, and participation became expected. Regardless of personal struggles, the emphasis was on serving the church's vision.

Over the years, I began to notice a pattern. New programs were constantly introduced, each one replacing the last, often repackaged with a new name. It became a repetitive cycle—measured more by success and failure than by true spiritual impact.

The church increasingly relied on man-made systems and ideas to drive growth. After spending ten years serving within this environment, I began to see clearly what was happening. These so-called purpose-driven approaches often misrepresented what the true church should be. There was little room for the Holy Spirit to move freely and reveal truth in people's lives. Instead, many leaders avoided addressing the deeper spiritual realities that were affecting people daily.

When it came to topics like spiritual warfare, many avoided the conversation altogether. When asked questions such as, *"Can a Christian have a demon?"* the responses were often vague, unclear or deliberately avoided. Scriptures were sometimes misinterpreted, and the issue was sidestepped entirely. This lack of clarity created confusion and left people without real answers.

In many cases, leaders either lacked understanding or chose not to address these issues. As a result, people remained bound, searching for freedom that was never fully explained or demonstrated. The system failed to acknowledge the reality of spiritual oppression, and many who needed help were left without it.

Over time, this became increasingly clear to me. As I matured and grew in understanding, I began to see things more logically and spiritually. I started to recognise the signs of a person who was bound and the deeper issues behind it. This awareness led me to grow in a new level of understanding.

Eventually, I stepped into a leadership role within the church, helping to lead in a home group setting. This position attracted a particular kind of person—those who were searching, struggling and looking for real answers.

At the same time, God was working behind the scenes—quietly orchestrating and realigning a relationship that would soon come into my life in a way that I could never have expected.

CHAPTER 12

A Sight For Sore Eyes

At this stage of my life, progress had become a defining feature of my Christian walk. I became more active within the church—serving, ministering and pursuing further study to develop my biblical understanding. I had a growing desire to help others, especially those who hungered and thirsted for righteousness.

This new sense of purpose was leading me towards my calling: to see people set free and to help them seek God for a better life. Yet, despite this growth, I carried serious questions about how the church operated and what it taught. Over time, I began to notice a repetitive cycle in its programs. Personally, I wasn't experiencing the kind of spiritual breakthrough I longed for. My heart still yearned for more—real answers and real freedom from the ongoing battle I faced.

Even so, life in the church continued as usual. I remained committed, serving faithfully in home group meetings. I genuinely enjoyed encouraging others and walking alongside people at different stages of their faith.

During this season, God began opening another door in my life—one I hadn't fully expected.

Within the church community, relationships naturally formed through shared activities and fellowship. Then, unexpectedly, something shifted.

There was an instant connection—a spark that felt undeniable. A beautiful young woman, already part of the group, was no stranger to me. But now, something deeper began to unfold. As we spent time together, it became clear that this connection was not by chance—it was God-orchestrated.

What began as friendship quickly developed into something more meaningful. I found myself drawn to her in a way I couldn't ignore. She carried a quiet strength, a gentle nature and a depth of character that captivated me. The more I got to know her, the more I realised she was far more than I had imagined—like discovering a treasure filled with beauty and substance.

For her, love seemed simple and natural. For me, it was more complicated. My personal struggles and the demands of my life made it difficult to navigate. Yet, despite the obstacles, I was determined. I pushed through distractions and pursued this relationship with intention.

As we entered a season of courtship, the relationship began to take shape with clear potential for marriage. It challenged me to grow—to make real decisions, adjust my priorities and step into a new level of responsibility.

Looking back, I can now see how this relationship aligned with the vision God had shown me years earlier—the image of a family. What was once just a glimpse had now become reality, unfolding in His perfect timing.

Our relationship soon became known within the church and among our families. It was clear that we were moving towards a shared future. This union felt divinely appointed—a marriage formed by God.

Despite this, we remained committed to the home group meetings. They continued to serve as a place of connection and encouragement, echoing the simplicity of early biblical gatherings where lives were genuinely impacted.

Life, however, became increasingly busy. Wedding preparations, home responsibilities and day-to-day commitments filled our schedule. My future wife continued working at the church for a season while we prepared for the life ahead.

This new chapter brought together two different worlds—culturally and personally. We both had to learn, adjust and grow as we built a life together. Whether at church or at home, our shared desire was to pursue God and build meaningful relationships with others who wanted the same.

However, beneath the surface, tensions remained.

The home group environment had changed significantly. What was once free-flowing and authentic had become structured and controlled under the church system. Many people began to lose interest. The very thing that once attracted them—the freedom to be real—had been replaced with rigid programs and expectations.

People were searching for answers, not systems. Yet what they were given often felt forced and disconnected from their real struggles.

At the same time, another issue was quietly unfolding in my life.

The *insider* continued to operate in the background. His intentions were subtle but destructive, working to confuse, manipulate and control. This ongoing pressure created a deep imbalance in my life. I struggled to function normally, constantly battling something I couldn't fully understand or expose.

This influence remained hidden—even as life moved forward.

Eventually, my wife and I made the decision to sell and relocate. She was excited to find the right home for us, and together we began the search. In time, we found the perfect place—one that felt chosen for us. It had character, warmth and a sense of promise.

As we settled into this new home, our desire to start a family grew. In time, that desire became reality—we were blessed with a child. The joy of parenthood brought a new depth of love and understanding into our lives. It marked the beginning of another significant chapter.

During this season, we continued running a smaller home group. Although attendance was modest, it remained a source of encouragement and growth for those involved.

As we matured in our faith, we became increasingly aware that we didn't want to settle for routine or repetition. I felt a strong conviction to return to the simplicity of the early church—gatherings led by the Holy Spirit rather than structured programs.

We decided to take a step of faith.

We began meeting in a new way—without agenda—allowing space for spiritual gifts, participation and genuine connection. It didn't take long before something powerful began to happen. People were experiencing God in a fresh and real way. There was freedom, authenticity and a tangible sense of His presence.

Momentum began to build.

But as before, opposition soon followed.

The enemy sought to disrupt what was taking place by reintroducing the insider into the group. One evening, he arrived uninvited with others, bringing subtle but manipulative influence into the meeting. Their words sounded spiritual, but something was not right.

At the time, we didn't fully recognise what was happening.

Looking back now, I can see how dangerous that moment was. Their presence disrupted the spiritual atmosphere, and the group began to lose its clarity and strength. What had been growing with freedom and power began to unravel.

Eventually, we slipped back into routine.

Around this time, the church introduced a new program centred on a book called *The Purpose Driven Life*. It was to be studied and discussed within all home groups.

But something didn't sit right with me.

I felt a strong conviction not to participate. During one meeting, I shared my concerns openly. I explained that the content felt more philosophical than spiritually transformative. This created a clear divide—either follow the church program or continue independently.

My stance was reported to leadership.

As a result, I was labelled as the problem.

The group was pressured, individuals were counselled and ultimately forced to choose. Under that pressure, the group dissolved. The weekly meetings came to an end.

This moment revealed a deeper truth—it marked the beginning of a new season.

With a young child and growing responsibilities, we made the decision to step back from the church environment and focus on our family.

Our absence did not go unnoticed.

One day, without warning, the senior pastor arrived at our home. His presence felt confrontational from the moment he walked in. After a brief greeting, he began speaking harshly—accusing me of rebellion, deception and a lack of submission to church authority.

His words were heavy, direct and deeply personal.

He declared that my actions reflected witchcraft and disobedience. He criticised my character and dismissed my perspective entirely.

I sat there in shock.

After everything—ten years of service—this was how it ended.

I didn't argue. I didn't defend myself. I simply listened in silence.

When he finished, we said goodbye.

And just like that, it was over.

After a decade of faithful service, my farewell was not marked by gratitude—but by accusation.

CHAPTER 13
Searching High & Searching Low

A few months went by, and my emotions were settling down after the disturbing, hurtful visit. This incident left me feeling humiliated and abandoned. I was happy to cut off **ties** and move on in life.

On one occasion, as it happened, we crossed paths at a shopping centre. The pastor approached me and, without any hesitation, quickly apologised for his behaviour that night, with humility. He said I was the better man in the way I conducted myself throughout the ordeal. I acknowledged him and kept walking. This careless incident didn't help my spiritual state; it just added more trouble to my struggle in needing to be free.

The church did have a system in place to offer help and deal with certain issues that would improve your spiritual state. These available sessions, which varied in topics, had aroused my curiosity. I would attend with expectation to receive something insightful, to steer me in the right direction.

After a while of hearing the teaching on this topic, it brought no fresh revelation on how to deal with this cause. They would only point out scriptural references to encourage you. The explanation lacked substance and did not demonstrate real power or authority in how to defeat the enemy.

This discovery didn't discourage me from pursuing other avenues regarding my situation. I even tried Christian counsellors, who might shed some light on this subject. I came out only to learn they operated in psychology-based approaches according to their training. I also attended programs based on special healing, where they would specialise in curses and blessings. With good intentions, I participated in this course with great hope, but afterwards realised I came out empty-handed.

I felt like I was wandering in the desert, looking for an oasis—my heart crying out for satisfaction. In this dry and thirsty state, I was searching for a fountain to draw from, yet not giving up in this wilderness. I still believed God was pointing me in the right direction, navigating me on this course.

CHAPTER 14

There's Light At The End Of The Tunnel

During that time, while I was still entertaining friends as per normal, it happened one day that a visiting friend had carried important information for me. In our conversation, she mentioned a pastor who could help with my situation. Upon hearing this, I was interested in meeting him and took down his details. The next day, I spoke to him and arranged to meet up for a coffee at a familiar shopping centre. I wanted to talk about what was bothering me and why I still couldn't find an answer.

After hearing my story, this minister wasn't fazed by this spiritual thing troubling me. He began to explain the reality of it all and how it operated.

This mystery made sense to me and I started to understand the reason for its continuous fight in this battleground of spiritual warfare. This is not taught or dealt with in the church—how to defeat this strange power. This spiritual discussion opened my eyes and caught my attention. It revealed the truth to a higher degree of knowledge that lay dormant within my heart and brought greater insight into this subject that still affected me. All my questions were answered one by one, as he explained why I was not winning this fight. This finally led me to believe this was the real deal. I was ready to come on board and work with him, looking forward to dealing with this issue.

Coincidentally, while sitting there and feeling happy to make this new transition of deliverance through this healing ministry, something began to shift in the atmosphere. The enemy wanted to cause hindrance to this road to freedom.

As a result, a mini spiritual battle began, where the previous pastor suddenly displayed a "sheep-stealing" mentality and called me at that exact moment. He wanted to make an extra effort in relation to my situation by offering helpful options available through the church, such as counselling. This phone call was an extraordinary experience, showing the lengths the enemy would go to use every means to divert me from the truth.

I was ready to be transformed. So, we set up our first session and began the journey to a new life. While we sat and talked, I noticed something different about his character. He had a caring heart and demonstrated the power of God by operating in the gifts of the Holy Spirit. Seeing this refreshed my heart, finally knowing there was hope. Step by step, through constant dialogue of questions and answers, he narrowed down the problem to deal with the source that was affecting me. He would pinpoint the root cause to break off the curse and whatever was attached to it. This relief came so naturally, without using brutal force, as the spirits showed no resistance in coming out.

The idea of being set free from this evil invasion, through prayer and authority, showed me a whole new dimension of deliverance. I experienced a new feeling of joy by the minute; it put a smile on my face and a song in my heart. This new understanding revealed a better way of casting out an evil force—through freedom. This special participation would evolve over time.

So, during my appointments, the common theme was continuing to allow the Holy Spirit to reveal whatever had a hold on me so it could be removed. This exercise of spiritual awareness showed me that these bondages wouldn't leave by themselves, but only through God's power—not counselling, psychology, medication or any other man-made ideas. This kind needed serious attention and had to be led by someone anointed and grounded in the Word of God. Someone who operated in the Holy Spirit, used the name of Jesus and commanded evil spirits to loosen their hold.

After so many years of struggle, I experienced the reality of this spiritual hold that continued to operate in my life. Although you read the Bible and say your prayers, it is not always enough on its own. You need teaching and knowledge in this area, so you don't become prey to the enemy, who wants to operate and dominate your life, leaving you going nowhere fast. This truth I had learned the hard way, by trusting people who interpret the Bible according to their beliefs and ignore the reality of it in their natural mind. They refuse to address the problem by dismissing its seriousness and take God's Word out of the equation, just to maintain a comfortable version of church.

It's not a matter of branding or singling out one church—there are plenty of good churches around that are fully aware of this issue. It was not hard to determine the nature of a church by listening and observing their terminology and where they stood on this topic. This major issue is often turned into a lie and prevents a person from succeeding when hearing statements like, "A Christian can't have a demon." One of the main reasons the enemy doesn't attack Christians is because they're not a threat to him. They can't expose him because they have believed the lie. It becomes easy to invent logical explanations—such as blaming the flesh, lack of renewing the mind or even not tithing—to explain away deeper issues.

No matter how it is articulated, it makes no difference. If a spirit has entered through sin, curse or ungodly influence, it will continue to operate and disrupt your life if it is not dealt with properly. A person must have both understanding and spiritual authority to see real results in this area, being led by the Holy Spirit to identify the source.

Because this subject is not taught correctly, many people remain in a state of struggle. They begin searching for alternatives, hoping to find sound doctrine and genuine truth based on biblical principles. Some fall away altogether, hurt and disappointed, turning their backs on God and convincing themselves He is not real.

The reality is, we often expect God to act according to our expectations—to come down to our level and remove all evil instantly. But sin produces corruption, and evil distorts what was originally good.

To experience the perfect love of God requires change and repentance. The answers are not found in temporary pleasures—movies, music or distractions—because these things can never fill the void. Only God can satisfy the emptiness within.

CHAPTER 15

Lay No Wicked Thing Before Your Eyes

By this truth, I can only speak from my experience. Having to learn the reality of good and evil on a greater scale, you come to understand how serious and dangerous the evil side can be. By playing with fire, they will ruin your life. This foundation has helped develop a greater awareness of what's involved and what steps to take in dealing with these evil rulers of darkness.

The way to improve my life in this spiritual war, I needed Godly weapons to protect and shield myself from the evil encounters that **surround** me. This exercise comes with discipline and practice, daily. To leave the old nature behind and renew your mind with God's principles, to overcome temptation and spiritual conflict. These personal battles can differ from time to time and it all depends on your faith level to win the fight. As the saying goes, 'it is easy to be bad but hard to be good.'

In my case, I needed to tread cautiously and weigh up my actions with spiritual awareness. Learning to be watchful and on guard, being able to distinguish the difference in whatever represents evil. This commitment to a new lifestyle became a serious matter when the spiritual opportunity would arise. Having to quickly adjust and spot the cleverly disguised spiritual **influence** operating behind the object.

After a series of trials in these typical events, I would fall repeatedly into old habits, weakness and temptations, where ungodly **pressures** would overcome these common factors that still lingered in my old nature, finding the struggle hard to resist. But practice makes perfect, as they say. I would start to take charge of my life and begin to filter out those wicked, ugly, detestable things with their subtle devices.

These things know our history and patterns—what we desire, what we enjoy and what we indulge in. They notice what tempts us and what our favourite pastimes are to get our attention. They deliberately set us up for a fall by distracting us from the truth and playing mind games. When something is played over and over in your mind, you start to believe it. The big selling point is to seal the deal by convincing you.

It all starts with images and enticing pleasures, which look pleasing to the eye and sweet to the mouth. These signs are carefully selected and displayed to target us. They use perverted instruments of disguise and place background images to sensitise our conscience and interest. They entertain us through television, music and video games, aiming to control us by creeping through the back door.

For example, have you ever seen the famous American Marlboro Man television advertisement? It is set on a sunny day in an open, wide country, with a cowboy sitting on his horse, looking free, cool and without a care in the world. He is wearing his hat with a cigarette in his mouth. This picture gives you the impression that when you smoke this brand, you too can be cool, just like him. This marketing technique made the company millions in sales by using this image and printing it on the packet. This cowboy died of lung cancer.

These illusions catch us out on many occasions, especially when they are formulated and crafted with religious figures that display foreign images linked to evil. These things are purposely aimed at the viewer, to attract them and connect some kind of spiritual influence through the eye gate that leads to the soul. When you experience these things, there is no doubt or confusion about their existence. You gain greater insight into the way they operate and affect people by exploiting their behaviour.

Deception is a clever tool when using an evil device to trap an easy target. By the time the victim wakes up to their scheme, the game is over—you've been sold a lie. To be entangled with the affairs of evil and taken for a ride, you're doomed to go down the wrong path without noticing. This feeling is all too real, where I was once bamboozled and confounded by the evil seed planted to occupy my thoughts, cloud my judgment and affect my ability to function properly. The constant torment refused to break, as I continued to push on and resist this evil.

There was no rest for me. Every day was a battle coming at me from every angle. There was even a time when the insider was still on the scene, hanging around and still trying to destroy and mess up my life. He picked an opportune time, with clever, sympathetic words, pleading to board with us. He wanted to stay in the bungalow at the back of the house. I was stirred with emotional confusion and didn't know what to say at that moment, but thank God my courageous wife stood strong and rejected this idea. He couldn't manipulate her. When he met with this resistance, he was not happy with the answer. Right there, I saw a different side to him, as he stormed out, cursing and hollering harsh words. Suddenly, I was relieved in watching him disappear. This moment revealed something questionable about him that settled my curiosity.

On a previous visit he made, I happened to ask him an important question: "How come you don't get attacked by evil?" He gave a very vague answer that concluded with, 'I was delivered long ago by listening to certain messages.'

This comment didn't sound convincing to me, and he became defensive. Then it dawned on me—how come I had done so much to be set free and yet I was still having this spiritual battle? The good news is, we didn't see this wicked person anymore, who was full of evil intentions, who served Satan and operated in devious schemes of destruction to ruin people.

It was a huge relief knowing this evil person was gone from my life, but the damaging trail he left behind, I was yet to see. For now, at last, all I could do was live one day at a time and concentrate on work, family and daily matters.

CHAPTER 16

Don't Bank On It

As the years passed, my immediate family was never short of problems. Whether relationships or money issues, one could see where it all stemmed from. History defines us through the trials of life. My siblings and I carried all kinds of deep wound issues that lingered through time.

On one occasion that involved money, a brother-in-law had borrowed a small amount from me, which in trust would be returned. Weeks had passed and the waiting game had escalated to more forceful attempts to recover what was lent out. I lent it based on my caring nature and willingness to help.

I am drawing a pattern here, to show how the evil one can use your current situation to lure you into temptation, by playing on your weaknesses, habits and interests. He will use this to his advantage, to create a lie by connecting the dots to a familiar situation and trap you into loss and failure. The evil one loves playing along and will carefully watch you. By taking note of your situation, he will then begin to implant cleverly disguised thoughts of opportunity and will use tactical devices to create false hope to the point of destruction.

This scenario of heartache happened to me—how, in one day, my life changed by making a hasty decision and acting upon a false impression where the devil planted a thought process that sounded so real.

This real-life event began on a normal working day. As I was stepping out to visit a site as part of my work routine, I suddenly heard a voice in my head, *"Call this lady about the money she owes you."* I didn't pay too much attention to where the thought came from, as it made sense regarding the money she owed me.

Without hesitation, I called to ask her about it. Her first reply was, *"How appropriate—you've called me at a perfect time. Can we meet to discuss a serious matter?"*

"Sure," I replied, thinking it was good news. But it wasn't. On the contrary, it was the opposite of what I expected. When we met, she shared a story of desperation and hopelessness, claiming she needed quick finance to avoid missing out on an inheritance that belonged to her friend. Without gathering all the information or history, I believed her and gave a large sum on the basis that it would be returned within a week.

This was not the case. I became entangled in this scam, becoming prey in a spider's web, as lies continued to unfold. One lie led to another, trapping me in a continual pattern of giving, with the promise it would be returned any day. This horrible situation became uncontrollable, as I was led astray to the point where my wife had a **breakdown**, and the flow-on effect saw me display the most uncharacteristic behaviour—gambling away our money on a promise of hope. Every action caused a chain reaction that placed strain on my marriage, work, family and friendships.

Credibility and honesty blurred the line between lie and truth. Eventually, after many attempts and seeing no return or benefit in chasing this ongoing cycle, it led me into a downward spiral of disaster. I was left empty-handed, broken and desperate, in a solitary place of deep depression. This experience truly shaped my perception and outlook on life.

I felt empty and bare, having lost so much, filled with questions and regret. To stop this cycle and seek help, I took a deep breath and reached out to a godly man for counsel—to impart wisdom, guide me in the right direction and help me deal with the painful effects of what had happened.

The process of rebuilding began—brick by brick. The first step was to repair my broken marriage. My wife and I came into agreement to stop this destructive cycle and refocus on our family, rebuilding trust again.

This also required a financial plan to work our way out of debt and to disconnect emotionally from this ongoing situation with these two women. Slowly, things began to improve. Little by little, signs of restoration appeared.

My amazing wife chose to stand with me. She was willing to return to work to help hold our family together. God blessed her, and she secured a job at her very first interview.

CHAPTER 17

Double For My Trouble

I continued working through the counselling sessions steadily, removing the weight of the world and the heavy burdens that held me down and kept me in a deep hole. I surely understood it was a little-by-little case, where the Lord was helping me rebuild my life. This included restoration and confidence to lift me out of this dark hole, where life would shine brighter at home, with financial stability to meet our needs, especially in the area of being able to borrow from the bank again, to clear up the debt.

As months passed, signs of normality were bringing us peace and assurance in our hearts concerning our marriage and home. This hope would dismiss the fear of loss and defeat that stared us in the face. Because of this predicament I was in, my spiritual affliction soared to another level, taking on burdens in every area of my life, making it hard to manage the weight of it all.

I was dropped in this dark valley, having to climb out of this slippery hill with one lifeline to rescue me. This ruthless attack became a struggle, in trying to function daily with no sleep and sanity. To carry this unbearable load was like falling in a deep well of torment. I felt like the man who is mentioned in the Bible that had a legion.

Week by week, my pastor would visit and deal with these things that had a stronghold over me. This process took time and persistence. Surely but slowly, we talked through the issues to determine every cause. Through prayer and deliverance, layer by layer, things would rise to the surface, exposing the lies I bought into. Every meeting became an eye-opener, with revelation and understanding that sin and curse were the cause in whatever situation I encountered, knowingly or unknowingly. In dealing with these curses that were operating in me through evil avenues, certain triggers would set them off. In this instance, something did happen.

It was the Christmas holiday season and during that time, we decided to go for a drive to visit family members who were enjoying a holiday by the sea. We took a road trip, heading towards our destination. This road was familiar, as I'd taken this road before with the insider. We finally arrived and spent some time with the family until evening. After that, it was time to leave, so we bid them farewell.

The next day, I was not prepared for this extraordinary experience. I woke up with this severe thumping in my head, followed by this agonising pain running continually down my left arm. It gave me no relief, nor would it allow me to sleep, causing me discomfort beyond measure. This was a mystery and I couldn't work it out. To find a cure in the natural, I tried a few avenues. Firstly, I sought out a chiropractor who worked on it, but the pain would not subside. Then I visited a doctor who, in return, prescribed tablets to reduce the pain. This helped to relieve the pain temporarily. But I still had this unbearable pain. I just could not pinpoint the cause. This strange feeling would not stop. It was a torturous week with no rest.

Until the day had arrived for my regular sit-down session with the pastor. I had the opportunity to share in detail this unusual pain that came out of nowhere. As we talked about it, we traced back my activities during the week and tried to make a connection to anything abnormal or unusual that might have happened to me that caused this painful adversity. During the conversation, the pastor suddenly brought a name to my attention — the insider's. When I heard it, my eyes lit up. Something stirred up that had been in hiding. This thing we had just discovered began to take shape. We traced it back to a certain time that caused this to manifest. It was when we travelled to this place. This encounter had revealed the source behind it. As I remembered, there was a time when I took a trip with the insider and saw him cleverly placing his hand on my left shoulder while driving. This was a form of contact that would deliberately transfer his evil scheme by touch. When this happened, I didn't take notice or suspect anything divisive in this action. I did find it peculiar, though, as I turned in surprise, but he just smiled.

This new discovery with the pastor had opened a window of deeper understanding about the power of darkness operating in the spiritual realm. This can invoke a curse and activate triggers that will set off the curse at certain times, making it a perfectly legal right to operate in your life.

This life-changing experience revealed to me how clever and crafty the evil side is, roaming around looking to target someone on purpose, to make them a vessel of despair by continually inflicting pain to the point of no return.

This spiritual involvement had a tremendous effect on me, leaving me to question its possibilities and what it can achieve through open doors. It is hard to comprehend or try to measure the depth of spiritual darkness that operates in people's lives. The spiritual world is beyond the realms of the natural mind. Only the Holy Spirit has the answer to every conceivable thing. Without the Lord, we are left to our own devices. If we don't do something about it, the evil will become a deadly poison to the soul and will produce sickness in the outworking of the body.

The truth will set you free. Taking on the challenges in our thinking and actions will give us the answer to our problem. Otherwise, you can't grow into the greater things until you get over the little ones. You don't get to a certain level and sit in a rut, not progressing.

As I learned about the spiritual side, this reality gave me greater insight into understanding how they can have legal rights in your life through ungodly means. This surprise came to me as I discovered that having certain items which represented the dark side — things like articles, pendants, ornaments, foreign objects, artwork or statues — these things, when given access, have the right to ruin you. As long as they stay there, you have granted them permission to occupy your territory and do harm.

I learnt the hard way, where the insider had put his dirty handprints all over our house, speaking all kinds of curses over our belongings, possessions and anything held dear to us. His intention was to divide and conquer. This evil practice had been in the making for years, deceitfully plotting his agenda.

This discovery explained the things that were causing all kinds of havoc in my life. So, I started the process of elimination. I began removing any items, curses, etc. that invited the evil presence in. This became my priority for release. This involved taking authority and breaking the power over every curse placed over our house and removing anything odd. This godly act closed the doors and the right to operate. By doing this, things started to improve in my health, finances and marriage. In time, release and freedom started to flow where restoration had begun. Favour and blessings were within reach, where once I felt God was far away and didn't care.

Battling ongoing spiritual warfare and lack of sleep was tiring, but now clarity and peace began to regenerate me, lifting me out of the pit of hell, to start functioning with a better outlook on life. It lifted my head and cleared the smoke screen of confusion and lies. It brought truth and gave me the ability to rise up with God's help.

It is true, when you walk in a dry and dark place, it is hard to see through the lies and emotional turmoil, where logic and reasoning have a detrimental effect on your state of mind, especially when finding no easy fix in this vicious cycle which you never asked for. The only good news was, I wasn't alone. God was on my side, which was better than having no one at all to call on for help. Being in restoration mode helps you define where you're at, and with every situation, you can reorganise that need. By pursuing and following the plan of God to rebuild your life, you will be blessed.

As I elaborated earlier, things began to take shape, as my darling wife got the job on her first interview. Call it luck or coincidence or just divine appointment. In any case, this opportunity helped us convince the bank for a top-up on the loan, enabling us to pay back our debts. And what was interesting, the bank waived our bad credit rating owed on the card.

As we secured more savings in six months, it helped us provide evidence and demonstrate our financial status to the bank. With this proposal, it increased our chances to start fresh. In doing so, we felt the time was right to sell and buy a new home, moving away from all the memories and dramas involved in this home.

We put the house on the market and, as favour followed us, we were able to sell within a week and find the right house that was awaiting us.

The new house we found had an interesting story. The house wouldn't sell on two occasions. This opportunity meant a better price for us, to meet our financial expenditure to the exact amount, and it was also close to shops and schools.

In the year 2017, there was a dramatic shift in my workplace. An announcement was made that the organisation had lost the government contract which employed about 500 people. This news left a lot of people in total shock and disbelief. After twenty-plus years of winning this contract, it had come to an end. This news meant that many people would be terminated. A redundancy package was given at departure. This chain reaction affected me, as I was a member of the organisation for twenty years. This emotional restructure of deploying staff had left people in a vulnerable position.

Grasping for answers regarding securing work again, with all this going on for me, I felt a sense of reassurance that God wouldn't let me down, knowing He was securing my future.

Meanwhile, as co-workers were being discharged, I continued to comfort them in time of need. The final day had arrived. It was an emotional scene for me, waving goodbye to the remaining work colleagues.

To comprehend this departure and decide what to do next in this puzzle of change, it called for time out at home, to reset and get a fresh look at different work prospects.

In doing so, I leaned towards operating a coffee shop as a small business. This idea required research and understanding in this industry. I needed to do some investigating. I was accompanied by my good friend, who had a wealth of knowledge in this area. The shop-exploring idea had plenty of possibilities for me. I had to weigh up and consider the opportunity. The only issue was, as time went by, the desire slowly diminished, leaving me wanting to try something else.

My next occupation came so naturally, as it was already birthed in me to become a handyman. I already had the basic instinct of repairing and fixing things. This profession was just a matter of getting started and setting up the business for work. Everything just fell into place in perfect harmony, without any hesitation. As I established myself with all the necessary equipment for service, I carefully took on small jobs to gain confidence in this field, to develop my skills and to get a better understanding of how things work over time. From the office to the outdoors, this type of job had the making of a willing person.

I am a people person, so I had no problem communicating with people. I had to tread carefully in how I treated and talked to them, because everyone has their own issues and a story to tell. I learned not to judge them by appearance, as you don't know what they have been through unless they share it.

This new occupation gave me the opportunity to connect with people and see where it led. Personally displaying a different behaviour and attitude compared to others in the industry. Spreading a little encouragement and a little joy goes a long way in the eyes of a stranger. This lifestyle reached a wider range of people who needed work done in their homes. This benefited both the customers and me, financially and relationally.

Of course, I had my own spiritual battles. Some involved certain people and some involved dealing with idols and spiritual figures on display within their domain, pertaining to their cultural practices. This didn't discourage me from earning a living. I understood what these characters can do and the evil they represent, which causes serious disorder in a person's life. There was only one way to learn and grow in this area. I continued to push on, regardless of the outcome. At the end of the day, I dealt with these things on the authority of the word that God promised.

Over time, I became used to expecting the unexpected when entering people's homes or having to face foreign objects. On several occasions, this had become part of my norm in this country. When you have experienced it personally and seen the results, who would dare to argue with your testimony? I am the standing evidence of a life-and-death experience, on every account.

As I later learned, part of today's revelations were things I encountered, like my first death threat, being in my country of origin when I visited my relatives with the intention of marriage in mind. But due to the incident of the horrific death of my father and his sister being killed by a bomb explosion many years ago, this injustice had filled vengeance in my cousins' hearts when they saw me. They planned for an opportunity to make amends for their mother's death by getting even with me. They believed my family was to blame for it.

When this news reached the ears of my uncles and aunties, they quickly came to my rescue and sent out a warning that there would be consequences if they brought any harm to me. This evil scheme they plotted fell apart, as I later found out.

On another occasion, it came to my attention that my nephew had got involved with the wrong crowd and was participating in their enterprises. This eventually caused a fallout due to his wrongful conduct, which led to a terrible outcome. The interesting thing about this situation was the head of this organisation happened to be an old friend of mine, who I grew up with in the old days.

By this time, I was already a Christian, so I gave him a visit and had a quick chat, which made him feel uncomfortable. By this time my nephew was in real danger, but for my sake he was allowed to go free. Later, I found out that a contract was put on me, but it did not come to pass because a higher power intervened.

In the year 2023, during a workday, I was walking back to my car when suddenly I became wobbly and couldn't balance myself. Not understanding what was happening, I assumed it was some kind of spiritual attack. When I got home, I started to hear a strange pounding sound in my right ear. It was an unusual condition that needed a doctor to examine me. To my surprise, the doctor performed all the tests and discovered my blood pressure was extremely high.

On that basis, the matter became urgent according to the symptoms. A head scan was ordered to identify the issue. Straight after that, I received a call from the clinic advising me to urgently go directly to the hospital. The test results showed I had an aneurysm, which somehow formed a dissection in the artery, making a bypass to the brain, which caused a minor stroke. This action could have easily torn the main artery in the back of my neck, leading to death. As a result, I was immediately put on medication and told to get plenty of rest and do nothing strenuous. The doctor was amazed at how I survived this incident. Slowly but surely, I recovered as I got my speech and memory back to normal. This episode proved to me that God has the last say and I wasn't meant to exit this world.

Another time I came home feeling sick and wanting to throw up. I thought it was food poisoning. Gradually I was getting weak and my head was spinning. I struggled to get out of bed. I felt motion sickness, like nothing I'd experienced before. During the night, I felt the need to throw up, so I forced myself out of bed and slowly walked over to the bathroom sink. This time I was worse off and dehydrated. In my fragile state, I leaned over the sink and threw up. Only this action took a toll on me. Suddenly, I fainted and fell over backwards on the tiled floor in our small bathroom. Some time later, I woke up and found myself covered in sweat, lying on the floor with my arm resting under my head. I did not feel anything, nor hit anything or injure myself. So, in my weak state, I managed to crawl back to my bed and lie there.

The next day, I visited the doctor with my wife and discovered that I had COVID. The doctor was in shock and alarmed when she examined me, because of my current health situation. Adding this on top could have been disastrous.

I gradually recovered to my normal state. This unbelievable episode that took place leaves no logical explanation for what happened. What remains is Psalm 91, which I decree and declare, that God's angels came to my rescue and cushioned my fall.

Over the course of my life, facing many trials and escapes, God's favour and blessing never ceased to amaze me. He's the promise maker and the promise keeper, who works together for my good and His glory and purpose. To grow in this ministry of deliverance and have a greater understanding in being able to determine the cause that controls a hindered person, who becomes a victim of circumstance by legal rights. Thank you, Lord. Amen.

QUOTES FOR THOUGHT

The valleys are deep and the hills are high. Where can I find pastures in the land of the living? I don't want to waste away by this affliction, or be cast down and consumed in toil all my days. What power can save?

The wonder of peace to grasp — where lie its chambers, and its source to draw from? Where to fathom its Prince of Peace?

This biblical principle of old had been put into action. As the saying goes, 'Build it and they will come.' Whoever thirsts and hungers for truth, come and draw this living water from the well, to refresh your soul in a mutual place of interest, bound by love to express the Christian way of life.

The way that deals with life issues where problems arise in a troubled, lost world. Come and find peace and godly principles to establish a good foundation and put them into practice.

I'm drowning here! It is a slippery slope, gripped by the clutches and the snare of evil. A pit has been dug for me without a cause in this dark and slippery pool of death. Who will reach down and pull me out?

All the fame and riches do not take the darkness out of my heart when I am a slave to sin.

What determines my condition is the words I speak, the life I live, and the actions I take.

Unforgiveness is one of the greatest bondages in one's life to carry, for it spreads its poison to take shape and form in its victim, to ensure their detrimental downfall.

Faith is activated by your actions.

Confession is good for the soul; it frees up darkness at the root cause.

Definition of a **BIBLE**: **Basic Instructions Before Leaving Earth.**

www.ingramcontent.com/pod-product-compliance
Lightning Source LLC
LaVergne TN
LVHW091012080826
845145LV00003B/1232

* 9 7 8 1 7 6 4 6 1 6 3 6 2 *